HISTORICAL AMERICANA

Michigan Faculty Series

The Quest for World Order, by Robert Cooley Angell
Law, Intellect, and Education, by Francis A. Allen
Thinking about Morality, by William K. Frankena

Historical Americana

BOOKS FROM WHICH OUR EARLY HISTORY
IS WRITTEN

Howard H. Peckham

Ann Arbor   The University of Michigan Press

Library of Congress Cataloging in Publication Data

Peckham, Howard Henry, 1910–
  Historical Americana.

  Includes index.
  1. United States—History—Colonial period,
ca. 1600–1775—Sources. 2. United States—History—
Revolution, 1775–1783—Sources. 3. United States—
History—1783–1865—Sources. 4. United States—
History—Colonial period, ca. 1600–1775—Sources—
Bibliography. 5. United States—History—Revolution,
1775–1783—Sources—Bibliography. 6. United States—
History—1783–1865—Sources—Bibliography. I. Title.
E188.P42 1980   973   80–13122
ISBN 0–472–06320–0

The chief source of spiritual nourishment of any nation must be
its own past,
perpetually rediscovered and renewed.

—Ralph Barton Perry

Acknowledgments

For help in checking titles and imprints, I am under foremost obligation to the staff of the William L. Clements Library at the University of Michigan, which library I also revisited on several occasions. I likewise made use of the libraries at Furman University, Appalachian State University, the University of North Carolina, and the University of Florida. The Henderson County (N.C.) Public Library was most helpful with interlibrary loans.

Several scholars have earned my gratitude for answering troublesome questions: Thomas R. Adams of the John Carter Brown Library, Richard A. Crawford and Allen Britton of the University of Michigan School of Music, Herbert Finch of Cornell University Library, Benjamin Franklin V of the University of South Carolina, Warren Howell of San Francisco, Charles C. Kelsey of the University of Michigan School of Dentistry, Mary Alice Kennedy and Sue Gillies of the New-York Historical Society, David Kirschenbaum of New York City, Paul Koda of the University of North Carolina Library, David J. Martz, Jr., of Colonial Williamsburg Foundation, William Matheson of the Library of Congress, John Shy of the University of Michigan, Clinton Sisson of the University of Virginia Library, Edwin Wolf II of the Library Company of Philadelphia, and Charles B. Wood III of South Woodstock, Connecticut. They are not responsible, of course, for my selections or commentaries.

Illustrations in this volume appear through the courtesy of the Clements Library of the University of Michigan. The cover illustration, "Clymer's Columbian press," originally appeared in Savage's *Practical Hints on Decorative Printing* (1821). It is reproduced here from James Moran, *Printing Presses: History and Development from the Fifteenth Century to Modern Times*, through the courtesy of the University of California Press (British rights courtesy of Faber and Faber Ltd.).

Contents

Introduction

*North Carolina Indian making a dugout canoe, 1585,
by John White, as published by De Bry in the second
edition of Hariot's Virginia, 1590*

Introduction

LL OF US know something about the early history of our country. We can recall the Pilgrims, the Indians, the Revolution, the War of 1812, the Gold Rush, and the Civil War. We can identify Columbus, Franklin, Washington, Lincoln, Grant, Lee, and a few other names. We learned these things, and more, from our history books in school. Maybe we did some additional reading of history or biography on our own. But the authors of those books—where did they learn all the facts they relate? How did they become so familiar with the events and personages of the past? They did research, of course, but what sort of things did they consult? What were their sources?

The historian's source material is the written record—printed books, government documents, letters, diaries, accounts, broadsides, newspapers, maps, etc. It is not what Aunt Harriet remembers her grandfather was told by somebody. It is not folklore. In general the historian seeks eyewitness accounts of events set down at the time they occurred, in manuscript or in print, by participants or close observers. He also wants the arguments about policy, the first descriptions of new areas, the transactions of organizations, command decisions in military affairs, sermons of revered ministers, and letters of faceless people. He is wary of autobiography and reminiscences of aging leaders; memory is selective, and time softens and alters recollections.

Source materials are not history; they are the instruments by which history is created. For the most part they are produced in the course of daily living for immediate purposes. What the historian does with those materials is to organize and interpret them for others. Since sources may not agree, any more than the witnesses to an auto accident, in evaluating them the historian must weigh evidence, examine causes and effects, trace influences, judge the competence of the reporter, and determine authorship and date if they are missing. Motives rarely are written down, so these the historian must reconstruct. He tests a hypothesis he perceives and forms his views into a closely reasoned exposition and narrative telling us exactly what happened and why. He creates "history," as we think of it. The essay or book he writes is a secondary work, not in a pejorative sense, but simply in contrast to a primary work, or source.

A significant aspect of source material is that it never wears out or is used up. It remains for the next generation of historians to use again, simply because it is all they have. Of course, additional source materials may be discovered, or formerly inaccessible sources may be opened to research. When that happens, they invite a revision of interpretation.

Secondary works are regularly discarded or superseded as fresh interpretations are published. Textbooks of a hundred years ago appear quaint, and monographs of similar age are no longer satisfying. We have queries they don't answer. It has been said that each new generation rewrites history to suit itself. This is true in the sense that new questions may be asked of old source material, and the results presented in new perspective and modern vocabulary. Thus it is vitally important that source materials be preserved and protected—which brings us to the collector.

The collector of historical sources is uniformed something like the historian, but he marches to a different drummer. He, too, is interested in his materials, but usually he specializes in selecting one type—printed books, or manuscripts, or maps, for instance—and he may restrict himself to a geographical region, a period of time, an event, or a person. Thus he may collect maps of the Great Lakes region, books on American medicine, letters from Civil War soldiers, anything relating to George Washington, or everything on Fort Ticonderoga. The choices and combinations are limitless. Where he differs substantially from the historian is in his attitude toward the sources he collects. Seldom does he want to use them in order to write a historical treatise. Making a collection is an end in itself, and in pursuing that end he educates himself.

The collector serves not only the historian but the bibliographer, the person devoted to describing accurately and completely the book or manuscript in hand as a physical object: its size, date, typeface, paper, printer, publisher, edition, collation, binding, number published, subsequent editions, and translations—everything that can be said about a book or manuscript as an artifact of its culture. The bibliographer also makes lists of related items, or describes all those titles bearing on a particular topic or area. For this information he is often dependent on the books gathered by a collector. His list is of immense service to historians, of course, and in turn to other collectors, who may be guided by the findings of bibliographers.

Where historian and collector begin to part company is over the latter's concern for the form and condition of his books. Not just any copy will do. The collector prefers to own the first edition. If it was bound when issued, he wants the original binding; if it was issued in paper wrappers or without covers, he wants it in that condition. Library stamps or perforations are defacements, and a book with pages or illustrations missing is a cripple. Provenance, or previous ownership, if distinguished, adds luster to a particular copy, and if the author or former owner has added marginal notes, so much the better. In contrast, some historians declare that all they want from a book is its textual information, and therefore a reliable reprint, a photocopy, or a microfilm is entirely satisfactory. The collector bears this heresy with whatever equanimity he can muster. He complains that such a historian has no *feeling* for his sources. He is correct in the sense that those historians who do have the imagination to become excited about first editions or original manuscripts usually communicate that excitement to their readers and students. Consequently, they are better writers and teachers than those who lack that enthusiasm.

The collector is entitled to respect, even academic respect, because he is primarily a conservationist and a connoisseur. Collectors in the Middle Ages kept learning alive by gathering, saving, and copying manuscripts. Their efforts helped make the Renaissance possible. Today the printing press has almost eliminated the possibility of lost learning through the deliberate or accidental destruction of books. Hitler's burning of books in the 1930s was the reaction of a fool; it availed nothing. In an occasional instance the first edition of a popular work has never been found, but more source books and scarce editions of the past might have been lost had it not been for active collectors. They are not mere gatherers of books or extravagant buyers, but experts in their fields, persons of taste as well as superior knowledge.

The following chapters are a combination of history, bibliography, and the lore of collecting. They attempt to identify and describe some selected source books for early American history, how they came to be written, their virtues and defects, their evaluation by scholars, how they have been used, and their appeal to collectors. Such books are not the only source materials a collector acquires or a historian uses, but I do not intend to discuss manuscripts, maps, or newspapers. The titles I shall examine are benchmarks in American culture, and I shall try to explain why historians and collectors prize them. Many of them are now so scarce and expensive as to be almost unobtainable, so in that respect this monograph cannot be considered a handbook for current collecting. Rather it is a guide for an excursion among the graphic monuments of the past.

CHAPTER ONE

The Discoverers

Le voyage et na-

uigation/faict par les Espaignolz es
Isles de Mollucques.des isles quilz
ont trouue audict voyage/ des Roys
dicelles/de leur gouuernement (z ma-
niere de biure/auec plusieurs aultres
choses.

Cum priuilegio.

⟨ On les bend a Paris en la maison de
Simon de Colines/ libraire iure de su
niuersite de Paris/demourât en la rue
sainct Jehan de Beauluais/ a lensei-
gne du Soleil Dor.

*Title page of Pigafetta's account of Magellan's
voyage around the world, as published in French
at Paris about 1525*

CHAPTER ONE

The Discoverers

HE HISTORIOGRAPHY of America has a precise beginning point, which cannot be said of Europe, Asia, or Africa. Exactly when written records begin for the Old World continents is hard to determine, but not for the Western Hemisphere. The first written reference to the so-called New World (it is Vespucci's phrase) had to wait upon the arrival of someone who could and did write. That person was Cristoforo Colombo (1451–1506), and the date was 1493.

The American Indians, with the possible limited exception of the Maya, could not write. Despite the high cultures developed by the Aztec and the Inca, the representation of word sounds by symbols eluded them. The woodland Indians of the eastern United States, the prairie hunters of the West, and the pueblo dwellers of the Southwest were all illiterate. As for predecessors of Columbus (to use the familiar Latin form), say what you like about the Irish settlement of Iceland, and the Norse who drove them out and went on to Greenland, and believe what you wish about the Welsh myth and the unlocated Vinland; it remained for Columbus first to make Europe *aware* of transatlantic lands—even though he was on his way to the Orient and believed he had found islands off the coast of India. Earlier sea ventures were fruitless because Europeans, lacking national states, powerful trading companies, and navigational technology, were not ready to expand and could make nothing of them.

Columbus was a native of Genoa and a man with a mission, both religious and commercial. Like so many visionary and determined men, he was immensely confident, even conceited. He took up residence in Portugal in 1477 after he had swum ashore from his sinking ship. Although the peasantry of that time considered the world to be flat, Columbus and everyone else with any education knew the world was round. Therefore he reasoned he could reach India, China, and Japan by sailing west across the Atlantic. Where he went wrong was in his calculation of the size of the world and hence the distance he would have to sail. He estimated that Japan must be about 2,400 miles west of the Canary Islands, instead of more than 10,000 miles directly by air. The reason he could not obtain financial backing from Portugal, Spain, France, or England for his proposed voyage was that those royal courts were advised by their geographers that Columbus's calculations were faulty, and that the distance was so great that a sailing vessel could not carry enough food for the crew on so extended a voyage. The monarchs were also turned off by Columbus's demands for a title, a share in any future trade, and a political appointment in any new colony.

Then Spain's Queen Isabella was persuaded by her husband's Keeper of the Privy Purse, Luis de Santangel, to reconsider and take a chance on this strange, obsessed Italian character. They underwrote the cost of outfitting three ships and saw Columbus off from Palos on August 3, 1492. He took on water at the Canaries and cleared them on September 6. Five weeks later he raised one of the Bahama Islands, went on to sight Hispaniola and Cuba, and found some peaceful Arawaks whom he named Indians because he was sure they were offshore natives of India. But of gold, silver, or jewels, there were none.

Leaving a few sailors in a fort (they were killed later), Columbus returned toward Spain, but was driven by a cyclone into the port of Lisbon on March 4, 1493. He brought back some plants, a few Indian artifacts, and ten Arawaks. From his log book he had compiled a report in the form of a letter in Spanish. It was not addressed to anyone, being more of a public announcement about what he had found and seen. It was forwarded to Ferdinand and Isabella from Lisbon presumably with a covering letter now lost. Columbus followed later, after anchoring at Palos and traveling eastward to Barcelona, where the monarchs were holding court. It was after the middle of April before he stood triumphantly before them.

The Spanish sovereigns had somehow made sure that the new Pope, Alexander VII, himself a Spaniard, was informed of the discovery and of the opportunity to convert newly found heathens. They also sought jurisdiction over those new lands before Portugal or some other country should assert a claim. Columbus's report was known in Rome before April 18, and a Papal Bull of May 3 quoted from it in confirming the lands discovered or to be discovered to Spain.

According to Samuel Eliot Morison, biographer of Columbus and historian of the discovery period, the sovereigns had manuscript copies of Columbus's report made and inscribed to certain court officials as a courtesy and in recognition of their interest. Luis de Santangel was given one, and it was printed as a four-page folio* in Barcelona. This first edition is so scarce that but one copy seems to have survived—and it is in the New York Public Library!

Another manuscript copy went to Gabriel Sanchez, the Treasurer of the court. One is tempted to regard him as a glorified CPA whose first concern was not what Columbus had seen, but whether the investment had paid off—and it hadn't. Be that as it may, the copy endorsed to Sanchez was

---

*Sizes of pages are given in terms of folio, quarto, octavo, duodecimo, and other Latin forms. They were not exact measurements but are based on the variable size of a handmade sheet of paper. Folded once, it is a folio, usually twelve by eighteen inches. A quarto is a sheet folded twice and is about nine by twelve inches. An octavo is folded again to about six by nine; a duodecimo is about five by seven.

translated into Latin by one Leandro de Cosco, about whom nothing is known, and sent to Rome in May. On the way it somehow passed through the hands of the Bishop of Monte-Peloso, in southern Italy, who added a postscript congratulating Columbus and King Ferdinand. The Latin translation was promptly printed in Rome by Stephen Plannck in an eight-page pamphlet of octavo size. Since Latin was the language most educated Europeans could read, the word was out of the great discovery. Four more editions followed in the same year.

Certainly it is an unpretentious pamphlet. If it ever had covers, they were probably plain paper wrappers. It doesn't even have the dignity of a title page. The first page begins with an introductory paragraph by de Cosco explaining that what follows is a letter from one Christopher Columbus "to whom our age owes a great debt, on the recent discovery of the islands of India beyond the Ganges," who had sailed "under the auspices and at the expense of the most invincible Ferdinand" (Isabella was added in the second printing). Then came the text, in which Columbus mentioned the islands he had found and named, the harbors, mountains, forests, the fertility of the soil, and the naked and peaceful natives who thought Columbus and his ships had descended from heaven. Columbus wrote that he was sure gold and spices could be found and declared he had taken possession of all those islands for Spain. Finally he rejoiced that so many souls existed to be saved. He signed himself with the promised title of Admiral of the Ocean Sea. Omitted from the narrative are distances and courses sailed, which rivals might follow, and any mention of the loss of one ship. He was intent on gaining support for a second voyage—and he did.

As indicated, the pamphlet is not much to look at. Some people are disappointed in its appearance and brevity, considering that it marked one of those corners turned in history. But as Dr. Randolph G. Adams, former director of the Clements Library at the University of Michigan, remarked, it was quite a lot for a man to write who didn't know where he'd been. The first Latin edition of three Rome printings in

1493—the earliest procurable edition today—survives in less than forty-five copies. It was, of course, reprinted in other cities and translated, until seventeen editions had appeared before 1500. Their order of appearance is disputed. Even fewer copies of the later editions can be found. Thus the news spread across Europe, which in its wake would never be the same again.

The copy of the first Latin 1493 edition most recently sold at auction (1966) brought $30,000 from a dealer, who subsequently sold it for $33,000. By no means is it the most expensive title in Americana, but it remains a very desirable book and the cornerstone of any respectable Americana collection. It has been reproduced and translated into English more than once.

Columbus's successful voyage and the lure of possible riches inspired other mariners, especially other Italians; the dominance of Italians in this activity is an interesting aspect of the Renaissance in that country. Amerigo Vespucci (1451–1512), a Florentine, clerked in the commercial house of the Medici family, and after 1491 represented the firm in Spain in banking and ship chandlery. He outfitted Columbus's third voyage. Vespucci wrote later that he crossed the Atlantic in 1497, but that trip was strongly doubted by Professor Morison. Indeed, his subsequent voyages provoke some questions, but it seems he did make a voyage to the West Indies for Spain in 1499–1500, and he went as navigator, not commander, on two voyages for Portugal in 1501–2 and 1503–4. His travels did not come to popular attention until 1503, when a letter of his was published as a pamphlet in Latin at Paris (where the translator lived). Vespucci's letter, addressed to Lorenzo di Medici, his former employer, described only his first voyage for Portugal to the coast of Brazil. The second edition (Venice, 1504) carried a title, *Mundus Novus,* by which the writing has come to be known. In it Vespucci boldly declared that the land he saw was not an island off Asia, but a whole new continent, a New World. In the next five years the pamphlet was widely reprinted in European cities.

Meanwhile, in 1505 or 1506 there appeared another Ves-pucci letter recounting four voyages to the New World. It was sent from Lisbon to Piero Soderini, a former schoolmate, and was published at Florence as *Lettera di Amerigo Vespucci*. If it is not the most reliable evidence of Vespucci's 1497 voyage, it must be said that it was not contradicted by his contemporaries. Columbus knew him and liked him.

The real significance of the *Lettera* rests on the use made of it by one particular reader. A copy reached an instructor in geography, Martin Waldseemüller, at the College of St. Dié in Lorraine, eastern France. Like all good professors, he was working on a textbook, an introduction to world geography. What he thought of Columbus, who still believed the West Indies were off India, is not known, but he was fascinated by Vespucci's entertaining *Lettera* and reprinted it as an appen-dix to his textbook. When, in 1507, his *Cosmographiae Introductio* was published in Latin at St. Dié, Waldseemüller made this suggestion:

> But now that these parts have been more extensively exa-mined, and another fourth part has been discovered by Americus Vespuccius (as will be seen in the sequel) I do not see why we should rightly refuse to name it America, namely the land of Amerigen or America, after its discoverer, a man of sagacious mind, since both Europe and Asia took their names from women. [I quote Margaret Stillwell's translation.]

The little book was popular and widely distributed, and the name stuck. It is not surprising that both of Vespucci's re-ports and Waldseemüller's textbook are highly prized by col-lectors of Americana, since they are responsible for the naming of two continents. The demand for them is frustrated by the fact that the four to six copies known of the three titles in first edition are all in libraries. The Waldseemüller was re-printed in 1907 in German and English.

Another Italian explorer, Giovanni Caboto, was a citizen of Venice, born probably in the early 1450s. He turned up in the great English seaport of Bristol in 1495, where he became known as John Cabot. The next year he and his three sons were authorized by Henry VII to find new lands, east or west, for England and themselves to exploit. Cabot planned to reach the Indies by sailing west along the shorter northern latitudes and going around any large islands. He left Bristol in May, 1497, and returned in August, after having bumped into Newfoundland. He raised an English banner on the north edge and followed the coast southward until it ran out. Perhaps he continued west to Cape Breton Island. Like Columbus, he thought he had found an island off Asia, so he sailed west again in 1498 with five ships—and never returned. Yet Juan de la Cosa's great map of 1500 in Madrid (though that date is now disputed) shows English flags down the eastern seaboard of North America almost to Florida! Could someone have returned from Cabot's last voyage? Certainly England eventually based her claim to North America above Spanish Florida on the strength of John Cabot's voyage, or voyages.

Cabot did not publish anything himself, but he was interviewed by Raimondo di Soncino, whose letter of December 17, 1497, to his patron, the Duke of Milan, was not published until the middle of the nineteenth century. The manuscript letter is in the state archives of Milan. Curiously, another letter of December, 1497, in Spanish, from one John Day, merchant of London, to a Spanish admiral, possibly Columbus, also reported Cabot's voyage. It was not discovered in the archive at Simancas until 1955. Both letters are secondhand sources, of course, and not the preferred foundation for history, but the Day letter contains an interesting inference that Bristol fishermen had seen North America in the 1480s.

Cabot's venture was first publicized in print when Richard Eden, an Elizabethan translator with a special interest in foreign narratives of exploration, compiled the first book in English on the discoveries of the New World. This was *A Treatyse of the Newe India* (London, 1553). He reviewed all the voyages across the Atlantic and advanced the claim of England to America by citing the findings of John Cabot. But the rival queens, Mary and Elizabeth, were not listening. It remained for Richard Hakluyt, geographer and promoter of English expansion overseas, to repeat the story and urge the claim in two works published in London in the 1580s before England attempted colonization.

Still another Italian discoverer was also a Florentine, Giovanni da Verrazzano (1485–1528). He came from a noble family and was well educated. To pursue a maritime career, he moved to France, where he made trading voyages to the eastern Mediterranean and seems to have known Magellan in Portugal. In 1523 he was allowed to use a royal French naval vessel to approach Asia by any strait he could find through the land barrier to the Pacific. To avoid hostile Spanish craft, he crossed the Atlantic north of the usual route and hit the American coast at about Cape Fear, North Carolina. He visited Indians ashore briefly, then coasted northward at a leisurely pace. Off the outer banks of Pimlico Sound he thought he saw the Pacific Ocean, since he could not descry the mainland beyond the inland passage. He went on up to New York Bay and dropped anchor between Staten and Long islands. Then he paused again in Narragansett Bay before passing along the Maine coast and turning homeward. He was back in Dieppe in July, 1524, concluding that there was no northern strait into the Pacific. Verrazzano wrote a letter to Francis I on July 8, but the king was at war with Charles V of Spain and could not afford to fund another voyage. Nevertheless, Verrazzano found commercial backing to fit out for a voyage to Brazil in 1527 and returned with a rich cargo of logwood, used for dyeing cloth. In a third voyage to the West Indies the next year, he was killed and eaten by native Caribs in sight of his crew.

The first printing of Verrazzano's letter to King Francis was long delayed. It appeared in Giovanni Battista Ramusio's third volume of his *Delle Navigationi et Viaggi* (Venice, 1556). The letter is the basis for French claims in America, reinforced by Jacques Cartier's voyage into the St. Lawrence River a decade after Verrazzano's journey. Although his voyage did not prove it, the Italian denied that Asia bordered on the Atlantic by insisting that the New World was not a long peninsula extending from Asia but a separate continent. He offered good observations of the Indians, and he also made a map. Hakluyt translated and printed the letter in his *Divers Voyages Touching the Discoverie of America* (London, 1582). Three manuscript copies of Verrazzano's letter are known today. One is in the Morgan Library, New York City; another is in the Vatican Library; and the third, a poor copy from the late sixteenth century, is in the Strozzi Library of Florence. A superb item to own!

These four Italian navigators—Columbus, Vespucci, Cabot, and Verrazzano—established the claims to the New World of Spain, Portugal, England, and France. (Portugal's claim to Brazil was substantiated by the voyage of Cabral in 1500.) Meanwhile, Ferdinand Magellan had demonstrated to Europe that none of the islands so far discovered was off the coast of India or China, and that not only was there a long and wide land barrier behind them, but another ocean, wider than the Atlantic, on the far side of that barrier had to be crossed before the Orient could be sighted. Suddenly the world was much larger than it had been thought to be. Concerning this remarkable man, Professor Morison declared: "Of the three greatest navigators in the age of discovery—Columbus, Magellan, and Vasco da Gama—Magellan stands supreme." It is a scholar's endorsement of what Americana collector Boies Penrose II said in 1953.

Magellan (ca. 1480–1521) was a native of Portugal, where his name is spelled differently. He became a naval captain and fought to establish a Portuguese colony in India. Later he aided in the capture of Malacca on the Malay Peninsula. In 1512 he saw the Moluccas, or Spice Islands. When he returned to Portugal, he was convinced that they could be reached more easily by crossing the Atlantic and the Pacific, whose width he misjudged. The trick was to get around South America, but Magellan believed the land must come to an end somewhere to the south. However, Portugal's King Dom Manuel I disliked Magellan and wouldn't listen to him.

Magellan also reasoned that if the line of demarcation between Spanish and Portuguese possessions in the Atlantic, as accepted in the Treaty of Tordesillas, 1494, were continued around the world, on the far side the Spice Islands would fall into Spanish jurisdiction. Spain should like to prove that, he thought, because Portugal was already loading rich cargoes there. So Magellan left Portugal in 1517 and laid his intriguing proposal before Charles V of Spain, a grandson of Ferdinand and Isabella. Charles bought the idea and arranged to give Magellan command of five ships and more than 280 men, one-fifth of the profits from trade, and the hereditary office of *adelantado* (governor) over any new land. A nice contract.

With courage and determination Magellan sailed from Seville in the summer of 1519. The expedition crossed the Atlantic to Brazil, turned southward, and laid up in a small harbor in lower Argentina for the southern winter. The decision was not popular, and on April 1, 1520, mutiny broke out among three of the five ship captains. Two were killed, and the third was eventually left behind. Magellan could be tough. One ship had been lost on the rocks, and later during the long passage through the straits that bears his name, Magellan lost another ship to mutiny when it turned back to Spain. He emerged into the South Pacific with three ships and ran north for a thousand miles before turning northwest across the equator and then straight west. He gave the calm sea its name, Pacific.

By bad luck the ships missed the verdant islands while their crews were dying of scurvy. Finally the three vessels reached Guam on March 6, 1521, and found fruit and vegetables. Ten days later Magellan made Samar in the Philippines and was peacefully received. He concluded a treaty with the ruling chief, and on April 27 he and his crew joined in a battle between natives on the neighboring island of Mactan. There Magellan was killed, along with forty sailors.

The leaderless survivors quarreled. One of the three ships was leaking and was destroyed. The other two sailed on to the Moluccas and were loaded with cloves. Weighing anchor in December, they became separated. One turned back and was captured at the Moluccas by the Portuguese. Only the

Vittoria, under Captain Juan Sebastian del Cano, crossed the Indian Ocean, rounded Africa, and reached Seville again on September 8, 1522, more than three years after embarking. Eighteen crewmen survived, plus four who were released later by the Portuguese.

Magellan had accomplished what Columbus had set out to do: reach the Orient by sailing west. The Ptolemaic system of geography, which had dominated European thought for centuries, reduced the size of the globe by thirty percent, and assumed a great continent south of the Indian Ocean, was overthrown. Magellan determined the correct length of a degree of latitude, established the true circumference of the earth, and proved the loss of a day in circling the globe westward.

Ironically, the expatriate Magellan's astonishing voyage established the longitudinal claims in the East of his ungrateful mother country. Yet the Portuguese empire declined during the rest of the century, while the Spanish empire flourished with its focus on Mexico, the West Indies, and South America as the continents took shape after the enlargement of the globe. Two other aspects of the long voyage are remarkable. One is economic: the sale of the cloves from the hold of the *Vittoria* paid all the expenses of the whole three-year expedition!—a revelation of the value of the spice trade to Europe. The other is historical: how we know so much about the incredible journey.

Magellan's sea journal was seized by the Portuguese in the Spice Islands and lost. If he wrote any letters during the voyage, they are not known. First news of the voyage to appear in print came in a newsletter of the Augsburg banking house of Fugger in 1522. Doubtless the news came from its Spanish branch. This pamphlet of eight leaves contained an inaccurate summary of American discoveries from Columbus through Magellan, but the latter's achievement is confined to the last paragraph. It is hardly a satisfactory source.

The second, longer account was the result of an interview. A young man named Maximilian, the natural son of the Cardinal Archbishop of Salzburg, was at the Spanish court under the care and tutelage of Peter Martyr, a resident Italian pedagogue, a member of Spain's Council of the Indies, and the first historian of America. Both pupil and teacher were on hand to hear the recital of circumnavigation by Captain Del Cano and one Antonio Pigafetta. Martyr then set Maximilian to write an account of what he had heard for his father as an exercise in perfecting his Latin. The long letter was dated at Valladolid, October 24, 1522. Apparently the proud father had it published under the title *De Moluccis Insulis (Of the Molucca or Spice Islands,* the wrong emphasis), first at Cologne in January, 1523, and later at Rome. It runs to thirty small pages and is, of course, a secondhand account.

Fortunately, Magellan had a passenger aboard, a tourist, who survived. He was Antonio Pigafetta of Vicenza, an educated young Italian who had talked the commander into taking him along for the adventure. It was this man who produced a detailed eyewitness account of the long voyage from his diary jottings. According to the custom of the time, he made or had made several manuscript copies which were presented to patrons and friends, who may have had additional copies and translations made. A version of the account in French, with the first two chapters of whatever Italian original the translator was using summarized, was published in Paris probably about 1525: *Le Voyage et Navigation Faict par les Espagnols es Isles de Mollucques.* It runs to 132 pages and includes a list of words in the languages of the Patagonians, Moluccans, and Filipinos, the first knowledge Europe had of these tongues.

Subsequent printings show a tangled bibliography. The French book was poorly translated into Italian, abridged, and printed in 1536, probably at Venice. Ramusio reprinted it in the first volume of his collection of voyages, *Delle Navigationi et Viaggi* in 1550. It appeared in English in Richard Eden's *The Decades of the Newe Worlde* in 1555, translated from Ramusio's Italian. A direct translation into English from the original French edition was not made until 1969, from the Clements Library copy.

The fate of the manuscript copies is even more fascinating.

Four have survived. An Italian text, though not Pigafetta's original, is in the Biblioteca Ambrosiana at Milan. It was published in 1800 in heavily edited form, then translated into French, German, English, and Spanish. The manuscript was re-edited in 1894 and revised in 1956. A better English translation, side by side with the Italian text, was issued in a limited edition at Cleveland in 1906. Two manuscript copies in the French language of different lengths are in the Bibliothèque Nationale, Paris. The longer one was published in 1923 and again, by a different editor, in 1956. The Hakluyt Society of London published in 1874 a new English translation of the 1800 Italian version amended with excerpts from the two French manuscripts.

A third French manuscript was found in a French convent at Nancy, passed into the hands ultimately of a noted English collector, and was bought in 1964 by Edwin J. Beinecke, who gave it to Yale University. It was translated into English and published in 1969. Several factors indicate that the manuscript might possibly be the very copy Pigafetta presented to Philippe de Villiers l'Isle Adam, Grand Master of the Order of the Knights of St. John, which Pigafetta joined early in 1524. For one thing, the early chapters are longer than those in the printed French version. Also, the manuscript had once belonged to the Cardinal of Lorraine, whose brother had devoted himself to the Knights and lived with them. Further, French was the official language of the order. The connection is intriguing. Pigafetta died in 1534 on the island of Malta, which was then owned by the Knights.

From this jumble of editions, which of the printed versions would a collector prefer to own? A good case can be made for the Paris edition of 1525, but the chance of finding a copy is remote. Up until two decades ago, only five copies were known: in the Bibliothèque Nationale, the British Library, the Biblioteca di Brera in Milan, and two in the United States, at the John Carter Brown Library of Brown University and at the New York Public Library. Then a sixth copy was found in France and sold to an English dealer in 1950, who in turn sold it to Thomas W. Streeter of New Jersey. When a seventh copy turned up at auction in London in 1958, from the Duke of Devonshire's library, it was purchased for £9,500 ($26,600). Later it went to the Rosenbach Foundation in Philadelphia.

In 1966, Mr. Streeter's copy, the last then known to be available, was sold for $56,000, in New York at the auction of his books, to the Clements Library Associates for the Clements Library. No commission was charged. Was that an excessively high price? It may have appeared so, except for two developments. Next day a disappointed private collector who had arrived too late for the sale offered the library $75,000 for it. Secondly, to universal astonishment an eighth copy of Pigafetta's 1525 *Voyage* appeared at auction the end of 1977. It was not nearly as a good a copy physically as Mr. Streeter's, but the bidding for it was spirited. At $75,000 there were still five bidders; then discriminating dealers began dropping out. The book was finally bought for Yale University at $130,000!!—again to universal astonishment.

In May, 1979, a ninth copy, from the same European private library as the eighth, was offered at auction. Having a repaired title page, it brought $100,000 from a dealer, presumably acting for an unidentified client. It scarcely seems possible that still another copy will come on the market.

There were other voyages, of course, and other reports of them. The books cited in this chapter are only representative, although they are high spots any collector of Americana would be proud to own. That fact is what drives up the prices. Further, they are prime examples of sources historians must use to construct the history of European expansion and the discovery of America. Most of them were written by the discoverers themselves, but for our age they need filling out, focusing, fitting into other contemporary events, and interpreting by scholars familiar with the period.

CHAPTER TWO

The Settlements

*An Indian village in North Carolina, 1585,
by John White, as published by De Bry in the
second edition of Hariot's Virginia, 1590*

The Settlements

HE FIRST ATTEMPT at English colonization in the New World occurred long
after Spain and Portugal had planted settlements in the West Indies, Brazil, Mexico, New
Granada, and Florida. It was largely motivated
by recent French expansion into North America.
Sir Walter Raleigh, a favorite of Queen Elizabeth I, sponsored a colony of 108 men who settled in what he called
Virginia on Roanoke Island, off modern North Carolina,
in 1585.

Among the leaders of the colony were Ralph Lane, governor; John White, artist; and Thomas Hariot, surveyor. The
last was a recent Oxford graduate; he had been a tutor to
Raleigh and was destined to achieve scholarly fame in mathematics. The colonizers were not happy in their new envi-
ronment, and they could not grow enough food or learn to
fish effectively enough to satisfy their hunger. When Sir Francis Drake stopped by on his way home from raiding Spanish
ships in the West Indies and sacking St. Augustine, the colonists asked to return to England. Drake took them aboard
on June 18, 1586. They had been resident on the island for
twelve months.

Raleigh was disappointed in their failure, and so were several of their leaders. He sent out a new contingent of 120

men, women, and children under John White as governor in
1587, but they were not supported from England as needed.
White returned home to get relief, but was delayed by the
Spanish armada's threat to England. One relief attempt in
1588 failed. When succor was finally dispatched in 1590,
White going along, no survivor could be found. Their fate
remains one of the mysteries of American history.

Meanwhile, to encourage further English colonization and
to counter false reports about Virginia, Thomas Hariot wrote
a detailed report on the region from his experience and notes
of 1585-86. He finished it in February, 1588, and it was
printed in London under a lengthy title that began *A Briefe
and True Report of the New Found Land of Virginia . . .
Directed to the Adventurers, Favourers, and Welwillers of the
Action for the Inhabiting and Planting There*. Of quarto size,
it contains forty-eight pages of information on "merchant-
able" products the area yielded, including timber and tobacco,
the foods that grew wild or could be cultivated, like maize
and pumpkin, the birds, animals, and fish, and "the nature
and manners of the Indians." He omitted any mention of the
growing hostility of the red men, and Governor Lane's attack
on the neighboring chief. Hariot concluded with the enthusiasm of a realtor that here was an Eden England should
develop.

This frankly promotional tract is the best description of the
wild region before white men began to despoil it, and a tol-
erant, favorable account of the appearance, behavior, religion, and government of the local Indians at time of contact.
The little book was popular and influential and still makes
good reading. Only five copies are known today: two in England, at Oxford's Bodleian Library (acquired before 1674)
and the British Library (obtained in 1846); one in the Nether-
lands at the University of Leyden Library, procured before
1716; one in California at the Henry E. Huntington Library;
and one in Michigan at the Clements Library, purchased in
1913. No other copy has turned up since then. The Clements
Library copy has been reproduced twice, in 1931 and 1951.

Not quite as rare is the second edition, which scholars have found more attractive because it is illustrated. While at Roanoke, John White painted a series of seventy-odd delightful watercolors of the flora, fauna, and Indians, and mapped the area. Done with close observation and considerable skill, the pictures rest today in the British Library. They were in the hands of White in 1589 when he was called on by an ambitious printer and publisher from Frankfurt named Theodor De Bry. The latter was the Henry Luce of his age, intent on launching a combination of *Time* and *Life* in a series of folio-sized reprints about America (a most timely subject), profusely illustrated with engravings made by himself and his sons from authentic pictures, and published in four languages so as to blanket the book market in Europe. De Bry wanted to inaugurate his *Great Voyages* by reprinting the Hariot booklet in English, French, German, and Latin, each illustrated by engravings made from twenty-eight of White's paintings. His dream was realized, and the De Bry Hariot of 1590 is a beautiful and highly desirable book, especially in English. Hariot added extended captions to the illustrations. It is also a milestone in science, because the work is based entirely on observation and is free from superstition and imaginary animals. (Incidentally, De Bry apparently overreached himself, because as he continued the series with twenty-six more reprints on America, he dropped down to two languages, German and Latin. All of the illustrated titles went through several editions, so that the New York Public Library has the series in 240 variants, a collection second only to the splendid one owned by the Earl of Crawford.)

The first permanent English colony in the future United States was, of course, at Jamestown, Virginia, in 1607. It barely survived after two-thirds of the original settlers died in the first year, and half of the newcomers the next year. The situation was made worse by quarreling among the governing council and widespread dissatisfaction among the commoners. Our best information about those early struggles comes from the colony's chief resident benefactor, Captain John Smith (1580–1631). He didn't mitigate his own role in helping preserve the precarious settlement, but his services can hardly be overestimated. A young adventurer at the start, he was not only courageous, but resourceful, diplomatic, and forceful, and both a good writer and a cartographer. In 1608 he sent back to London a manuscript about Virginia which was printed as A True Relation of Such Occurrences and Accidents of Noate as Hath Hapned in Virginia. . . .

Smith returned to England in October, 1609. Three years later he published A Map of Virginia, with a Description of the Countrey, the Commodities, People, Government and Religion (Oxford, 1612). The work contained as much on the Indians as on the new English settlement. Returning to America, he explored and mapped the New England area, publishing another book which was used by the Pilgrims who landed at Plymouth in 1620. Then Smith wrote his Generall Historie of Virginia, New-England, and the Summer Isles (London, 1624), which included most of his earlier writings. It was not until this book that he related the story of his life being saved, while a prisoner of Powhatan, by the intercession of Pocahontas, young daughter of the chief. Smith also recounted the Indian uprising of 1622 that nearly wiped out the colony.

Smith's books are source materials of the highest order, having been written by the leading protagonist while his experiences were fresh in his mind. To be sure, they reflect his views, but nothing else can take their place. Other men wrote about Virginia, too, and all of their works are sources for the history of our oldest state.

The French experience paralleled that of the English, although it started somewhat earlier. After Verrazzano, Jacques Cartier (1491–1557) carried the French flag into the Gulf of St. Lawrence in 1534. His report of a warmer climate than previously believed led the king to send him back in 1535, when he ascended the St. Lawrence River past the mouth of the Saguenay and up to Hochelaga where he named the hill Mount Royal (Montreal). In 1541 he was back again to help the Sieur de Roberval with a colonization scheme that failed. Cartier wrote on account of his explorations in Brief

Recit, & Succincte Narration, de la Navigation Faicte es Ysles de Canada (Paris, 1545). It is a small octavo of less than a hundred pages containing much information about the Indians along with geographical description. It was translated into Italian and published by Ramusio in his 1556 anthology. The English edition of 1580 is a translation from Ramusio, as (probably) is the Rouen French edition of 1598. The original was reprinted at Paris in 1863, and the best English edition appeared in 1924.

The second attempt at French colonization was made in 1562 by a French admiral who sent a Huguenot (Protestant) group to Parris Island, South Carolina, under Captain Jean Ribaut. As in the case of Roanoke, the colony was poorly governed, and everyone grew discouraged. After a few months they returned to France. Ribaut had tried earlier to procure reinforcements from France, but found Catholics and Protestants at war with each other, and early in 1563 he went to London, where he wrote an account of his colony. If it was published in French, no copy is known; but it appeared in English translation as *The Whole and True Discoverie of Terra Florida* (London, 1563). It is of legendary rarity, only two copies being known, and both are in England. The book was reproduced in facsimile by the Florida State Historical Society in 1927.

However, in 1564 a second attempt at colonization by Huguenots was made under Lieutenant René de Laudonnière (1529–1574), who had been in the first colony. He stopped at Parris Island, then moved southward to present-day Jacksonville, Florida, and built Fort Caroline. With him was Jacques Le Moyne, an artist. The new location was close to the Spanish Main, where treasure ships passed on their way to Spain filled with Mexican and Peruvian silver and gold. Some of the French colonists took a ship and, in search of quick wealth, raided Spanish galleons, an act of piracy and extreme foolishness, for Spain was bound to retaliate.

With reinforcements, Captain Ribaut returned to Florida in 1565 to take command. Hearing of a Spanish landing in a harbor thirty-five miles south (at St. Augustine), Ribaut took most of his force to attack it, but his ships were scattered and wrecked in a tropical storm. The Spaniards then marched up the coast to drive out the French "heretics." They had no trouble capturing Fort Caroline, and after the French were promised good treatment if they surrendered, almost all were killed. Laudonnière, though wounded, and Le Moyne and a few others escaped and got back to France. Meanwhile, Ribaut and his surviving men had been captured and killed. The bloody exchange was not finished: three years later another Frenchman retook Fort Caroline and slaughtered all of the Spanish garrison. But French colonization in this region ceased.

These futile efforts were related in three accounts. A carpenter named Nicolas Le Challeux wrote or told someone of his adventure in the Spanish massacre. His narrative was printed in his hometown under the title of *Discours de l'Histoire de la Floride, Contenant la Trahison des Espagnols, Contre les Subiets du Roy* (Dieppe, 1566). Running to fifty-four pages, it was reprinted several times and translated into English, German, and Latin.

Laudonnière found himself discredited in France and wrote a defensive account of everything that had happened to the ill-fated Florida colony. The manuscript seems to have been lost or suppressed until years after Laudonnière's death. Richard Hakluyt found it during a visit to Paris and urged its publication. It came out as *L'Histoire Notable de la Floride Située es Indus Occidentales* (Paris, 1586) and included an account of the final French revenge at Fort Caroline. It was translated into English and published the next year in London; the original was reproduced in facsimile in 1964.

Meanwhile, Jacques Le Moyne, who settled in London, prepared a narrative to go with his watercolors and drawings of Florida. While De Bry was in London to contract with Hariot and White, he tried to persuade Le Moyne to let him publish the narrative with illustrations, but failed. After the Frenchman's death, De Bry bought the manuscript and pictures from the widow, and Le Moyne's work was published in 1591 as the second volume (after Hariot) in De Bry's *Great*

Voyages, in Latin and German. The Latin title began *Brevis Narratio Eorum que in Florida* and was illustrated with forty-two plates from the brush of Le Moyne.

After the failure in Florida, four decades passed before an indifferent French king gave a fur-trading monopoly in America to another Huguenot, the Sieur de Monts, in 1604. The latter employed Samuel de Champlain (ca. 1570–1635), a Catholic naval officer and royal geographer, to establish a post the next year on the south side of the Gulf of St. Lawrence in Arcadia, or Nova Scotia, well away from the Spaniards. Champlain was selected because he had visited the area in 1603 as an adventurer with a friend's exploratory voyage and had sailed up the St. Lawrence, the Saguenay, and the Richelieu rivers "more than 450 leagues." He witnessed several Indian ceremonies, and on his return to France wrote and published *Des Sauvages, ou, Voyage de Samuel Champlain* (Paris, 1603), an account of the customs and manners of the Algonquins, the animals, trees, fruits, rumors of mines, and the coast of Arcadia (the name was corrupted later by dropping the *r*). Champlain's colony lasted less than three years, during which time he explored down the Maine and Massachusetts coast to Cape Cod. Then in a revulsion against the Protestants France revoked de Monts's privilege, and the colony was abandoned.

However, Champlain had become enchanted by the region, and in 1608 he persuaded the king to permit him to found a colony in a new location. Accordingly he brought twenty-eight settlers up the St. Lawrence and on a rocky ledge established Quebec and sustained it, although nineteen died during the first winter. He also invaded modern New York and discovered the lake that bears his name. In 1611 he cleared a site for another post upriver where Montreal ultimately was established, and founded Trois Rivières, halfway between Quebec and the Montreal site. After he returned to France to seek more support he wrote of his Canadian venture in *Les Voyages du Sieur de Champlain,* illustrated with maps he had drawn. It was published in Paris in 1613, and with it the continuous history of New France, or Canada, begins. The book is rich in description of the eastern region and its settlement, the fish and fur, the Algonquins and their enemy the Iroquois, and the progress of missionary activity which Champlain initiated.

In 1619 a second edition was published under an altered title; it recounted his western exploration up the Ottawa River in 1615 with some Hurons, who took him to their villages on Georgian Bay of Lake Huron. A third edition, under a slightly different title, appeared in 1632, bringing the history down to that date.

The first account of the English Pilgrims at Plymouth is credited to "the little man who wasn't there"—G. Mourt. George Mourt was converted to Puritanism in England and moved with the Separatists to Holland, where he prospered as a merchant. In 1619 he returned to England and changed his name to Morton, possible so as not to embarrass his Catholic relatives. He did not migrate to Plymouth until 1623, and meanwhile served the Pilgrims' interests at home. In 1622 he received reports on the new settlement from Governor William Bradford and Edward Winslow and took them to a printer. Whether he did any writing or editorial work, or merely served as publisher, is not certain, but the book came out under his old name with the title *A Relation, or Journall of the Beginning and Proceedings of the English Plantation Settled at Plimouth, in New England* (London, 1622).

Like Hariot's book, it was designed to attract more colonists. It praised the climate and the fertility of the soil as well as the bounty of the sea and forest, reviewed the achievements of the settlers, and advised prospective emigrants on what stores to take with them. In some detail the book told of the *Mayflower* voyage, the wanderings of the Pilgrims around Cape Cod, the building of Plymouth, the helpfulness of the Indians, and the first Thanksgiving. Although mention was made of the Christian's duty to convert the Indians, the authors well knew that the prospect of economic improvement was the most potent motivation to future settlers in the face of unemployment and limited opportunity in England. The theme of America, the land of opportunity, was born. Work was plentiful and would be rewarded.

The other great source on Plymouth is Governor Bradford's history, which did not get published for more than two hundred years. It covers the Separatists in Holland, the business arrangements with sponsors for an overseas move, the voyage of the *Mayflower,* the hard times and quarrels, relations with the Indians and the Pequot war, the beaver trade, occasional crime, news from the London partners, etc. It continues chronologically through 1646 and includes a list of the *Mayflower* passengers with a summary of their marriages and deaths, as well as the Compact they signed for self-government. Meanwhile Boston was founded by other Puritans in 1630, settlements were established in Rhode Island and Connecticut, and Plymouth itself sponsored ten satellite hamlets.

Bradford's manuscript descended to a son and grandson, and it was consulted by several pre-Revolutionary historians of New England. The last one, Thomas Prince, borrowed it, and upon his death in 1758 it went with his other books to the library in Old South Church, Boston. Part of that library was taken away by the British when they evacuated Boston in 1776. Somehow it crossed the Atlantic and ended up in the possession of the Lord Bishop of London, where it was rediscovered in 1846. It was first published by the Massachusetts Historical Society in 1856 (with sixteen lines inadvertently omitted). In a generous gesture the original manuscript was given to the state of Massachusetts in 1897 and was published again by order of the General Court in 1901, with an index. The title Bradford used is "Of Plimoth Plantation," but it is commonly known as the Bradford History. Samuel Eliot Morison edited it again in 1952, adding an introduction and notes.

Other early settlers of Massachusetts Bay wrote of the new country and their experiences, but Mourt's and Bradford's titles are basic for the story of first settlement. Owing to its late printing, the Bradford History of 1901 or 1952 is an example of a source that is neither scarce nor expensive, in contrast to Mourt's *Relation*. The difference illustrates another distinction between the collector and the historian: the historian may consider the Bradford History as valuable a source as the Mourt *Relation,* or even better, but the collector finds the Mourt much more desirable because it is so scarce. (Thomas Streeter's copy sold for $16,000 in 1967.) The collector doesn't despise the Bradford, but ownership of it is so easy it confers no particular satisfaction. This attitude, whatever one may think of it, explains a dealer's definition of a rare book: it "is important, desirable, and *hard to get.*"

Henry Hudson was looking for something else when he sighted the river that bears his name. An English navigator, he had tried to find a sea route to the East around northern Europe. Failing that, he engaged himself to the Dutch East India Company in 1609 for a similar quest. Naturally, he failed again, and in frustration he violated his instructions by crossing the North Atlantic. He coasted south along the shore of North America looking for a northwest passage around the continent. In September, 1609, he entered New York Bay and in the *Half Moon* ascended the river almost to modern Albany. If he had gone a little farther and seen the Mohawk River pouring in from the west, no doubt he would have felt there was a waterway to the Pacific. But he returned to England and sent a report to his employers in Holland, giving that country its claim to the Hudson River region, although the area lay within the vague English claim of Virginia.

Hudson's life ended tragically. Another voyage, sponsored by English merchants, carried him into the great bay named for him, where he wintered with a hostile crew. In the spring of 1611 the sailors mutinied under the leadership of Robert Juet and set Hudson, his son, and seven loyal crewmen adrift in a small boat with no supplies. They certainly perished soon afterward. But England had its claim to the whole Hudson Bay area, sandwiching France's domain between that and Virginia.

We know all this primarily from two sources. Emanuel van Meteren (1535–1612) published a book in 1610 about Dutch explorations. The next year in a new edition under a new title, *Belgische ofte Nederlantsche Oorlogen ende Geschiedenissen,* a quarto of more than 700 pages, appeared the first printed account of Hudson's voyage for the East India Company. It was reprinted in 1614. Then Robert Juet, the villain in Hudson's death, luckily died himself on his return to England from the mutiny. He left a diary, kept like a log book, of Hudson's earlier voyage into New York Bay and up the river. It was preserved by that noted collector-editor, Richard Hakluyt, who gave it with other papers as a bequest to his friend Samuel Purchas. The latter published it in the third volume of his anthology called *Hakluytus Posthumus, or Purchas His Pilgrimes* (London, 1625).

Two other sources, likewise Dutch and English, carry on the story of New York. Adriaen van der Donck's *Beschryvinge van Nieuw-Nederlant* (Amsterdam, 1655) celebrates the settlement of the colony called New Netherland. It is a hundred-page book descriptive of the nature and productivity of the colony and the opportunities for profit. It contains an engraved view of New Amsterdam on Manhattan Island. Popular enough to be reprinted the next year, the second edition omitted the engraving and offered a Visscher map of the area. The work was translated for the New-York Historical Society's *Collections,* second series, Volume 1 (1841).

The colony did not prosper, however. In 1614 a dozen Dutch shipowners had sponsored a trading post at Fort Nassau, far up the Hudson on an island near modern Albany, to obtain furs from the Iroquois. No settlement was made, and the trade monopoly obtained was good for only three years. Finally in 1621 the Dutch government chartered the West India Company, which could establish a colony, govern it, enjoy a trade monopoly for twenty-four years, sell stock, and license traders. The first director general led some Walloons to New Netherland in 1624; some of them erected a fort on modern Governor's Island, while others constructed Fort Orange at modern Albany to replace Fort Nassau, washed out in a flood. A second wave of immigrants came in 1625, settled on Manhattan, and built a fort. The place was called New Amsterdam. The new director general bought the island from the Indians for sixty guilders—equal to $24, the figure of enduring fame.

So far from promoting growth, the West India Company was interested only in the fur trade and big dividends. Prosperity and religious toleration at home, in contrast to England, discouraged migration. The company resorted to making grants of large tracts of land along the Hudson to any stockholder who would settle fifty adults on it—the patroon system. It was notably unsuccessful. The company then tried to develop its own farms, or bouweries, tenanted by indentured servants. Meanwhile, some English settlers had moved onto the eastern end of Long Island.

War between England and Holland developed in 1652–54, but left New Netherland unaffected. Not having to concentrate on defense, the unpopular director general, Peter Stuyvesant, moved against the Swedish settlements on the Delaware River in 1655 and captured them. But in 1664 an English squadron seized New Amsterdam, largely because the Dutch inhabitants would not support Stuyvesant's resistance. The treaty of 1667 confirmed the victory. At that time New York, as it was renamed, had a population of only about eight thousand Hollanders, Flemings (who spoke a Germanic Dutch), Walloons (who were essentially French), and English. New York's cosmopolitanism was already well established. English became the language of commerce and government, and only the Dutch Reformed churches remained as the last bastion of the Dutch language in America until the Revolution.

The first separate account in English regarding New York was the work of Daniel Denton, a planter and public official, whose father was a Presbyterian minister on Long Island. He was visiting London in 1670 when he wrote *A Brief Description of New-York, Formerly Called New-Netherlands.* Denton recommended the fertility of the soil, the healthiness of the climate, the good crops, and the Indians, and gave advice to new settlers. He tended to emphasize Long Island, with which he was most familiar. About two dozen copies of his tract are known today. Under English rule the colony attracted artisans and merchants not concerned with Puritanism or tobacco plantations.

New York found its first historian in William Smith, Jr. (1728–1793), a Yale graduate, attorney, and Loyalist chief justice of the colony. He wrote *The History of the Late Province of New-York, From its Discovery, to the Appointment of Governor Colden, in 1762,* in two volumes. The first, running to 1732, was published at London in 1757; the second did not appear until the New-York Historical Society published it along with a reprint of the first volume in 1830. Smith moved to England after the Revolution and then settled in Canada.

Every American colony has a distinctive history and its own source material. From these sources the historian can reconstruct the numerous happenings in each location and trace the growth of our heritage. The language of the time doesn't have quite the same impact on late twentieth-century readers that it had on contemporaries of the authors. Rewriting and interpretation are essential, though the sources are constant.

CHAPTER THREE

Religious Innovations

Separate print of Shakers dancing at their community
near Lebanon, New York

CHAPTER THREE

Religious Innovations

HE AMERICAN INDIAN was not only a surprise to Europeans because of his unimagined color and his Stone Age culture, but a shock to some of their religious assumptions. The natives of the West Indies and the southern United States seemed to demonstrate that not all men had been condemned to toil and suffering for some inherent original sin. Those Indians lived easily on nature's bounty, with little work, in shameless nakedness, and apparently free of wars. Gradually the Europeans found their view of this idyllic, if disturbing, life was not entirely accurate. Yet it suggested that man's nature was not so much responsible for his unhappiness as some fault in his social organization and some defect in his climate. At least it appeared that he was not universally damned to misery, a radical idea in itself. Other unorthodox religious ideas developed in the course of colonizing the New World.

There is no such thing, of course, as an American religion, only American contributions to Christian thought and practice, some of which launched new sects. The colonies that formed the United States were predominantly Protestant and British. In fact, even by 1775 over 98 percent of the inhabitants were Protestant, and nine out of ten were British. The chief denominations on the eve of the Revolution were Congregational, Presbyterian, Anglican, Baptist, and Friends, and this diversity represented a triumph of tolerance not present at first.

What was American about organized Protestantism was twofold and began with the New England Puritans. The first Puritans of England wanted only to "purify" the Church of England of certain rituals and attitudes that seemed too formal and Biblically unjustified. But those who migrated not only were bound on a holy mission, but added a new dimension by separating themselves geographically from king and bishops. The Massachusetts Bay Puritans were Anglican nonconformists originally, not conscious Separatists like the Plymouth Pilgrims, but they could find authority only in their own charter and congregations. To justify self-governing churches, a covenant theology was emphasized—that is, any body of believers could enter into a direct relationship with God and with one another on a kind of contractual basis. If men would but believe in Him, He would show them how to receive divine grace and achieve salvation. Two developments followed: "any body of believers" meant, in time, tolerance of differing bodies; and "the priesthood of all believers," implicit in a sovereign congregation, caused bishops to be regarded with indifference, then suspicion, and finally hostility.

The first idea would eventually encourage splinter groups rather than preserve orthodoxy, as shall be seen. The latter idea spread southward to Anglican churches, whose memberships divided over the advisability of having an American bishop, and none was ever appointed before the Revolution. Those Puritans who felt some hierarchy of authority desirable became Presbyterians and gave allegiance to presbyteries, synods, and a general assembly, all democratically organized. The Congregationalists and Baptists stuck to the sovereignty of their separate churches, and the Quakers pulverized even that much autonomy by recognizing the individal conscience as supreme. As a further distinction from Anglicanism, all of them elevated the pulpit over the altar, making the sermon, which was explication of Scripture, the preeminent part of the Sunday service. One effect of this emphasis was ardent support for schools and colleges to confound Satan by providing a true knowledge of the Bible from educated clergymen.

The other American contribution had to do with the church's relation to government. In England the king was head of the established Anglican church and appointed its archbishops and bishops. They in turn assigned priests to particular parishes. Moreover, an "established" church meant that all these clergymen were paid by the government from tax revenues. But in America, if congregations were sovereign, they not only might hire their own ministers but eventually must pay them. A minister's authority came not from his office but from his character and ability. Paying ministers from member offerings did not take root at once, and in several New England colonies the Congregational church was established by granting it state tax monies for operations. When other denominations were not so favored, they objected and eventually ended the subsidy to any church. Civil magistrates were freed of clerical supervision and of trying to impose church policies on nonmembers. Similarly, the self-sustaining church was free to criticize the government. Church and state were separated forever in this country.

In retrospect we can see these American ideas taking root in the clash of two Puritan personalities: John Cotton and Roger Williams. John Cotton (1584–1652) was a Cambridge-educated Anglican priest who became a quiet Puritan and gradually instituted in his church in Boston, Lincolnshire, certain nonconforming and simpler forms of worship. When he was called to London to face discipline, he resigned and fled to Massachusetts in 1633 where he became "teacher" of the Boston church. There he found kindred souls and at first took a liberal stand on church membership, allowing anyone who was "Godly" to join without having to renounce the Anglican church. Here he was taken to task by Roger Williams, who was hostile to the Church of England. Cotton defended his parishoner, Mrs. Anne Hutchinson, who was alarming the clergy by suggesting that a truly saved or regenerate individual could tell intuitively whether others, including ministers, were truly regenerate; but when he discovered that most of his clerical colleagues wanted to banish her for setting the Holy Spirit above the Bible, he joined them.

At heart Cotton was not a Separatist. From his Anglican background he could not shake off the belief that civil magistrates, as long as they were Puritans, should have authority over religious as well as secular affairs. He had no faith in the wisdom of the common man. "Democracy," he once said, "God did not ordain as a fit government either for church or commonwealth." In the end he opted for state authority to enforce conformity. Yet he extolled the methods of Congregationalism in two popular treatises. He also prepared a catechism for children called *Milk for Babes, Drawn Out of the Breasts of Both Testaments* (London, 1646). It was reprinted in Boston in 1656 under the delightful title *Spiritual Milk for Boston Babes in Either England*. It was considered good enough to be translated and published for the Natick Indians, west of Boston.

At the same time Cotton became embroiled in a second dispute with Roger Williams (1604–1683), perhaps the most radical preacher of the day. Williams had migrated to Boston in 1631 and earned the displeasure of the theocratic Massachusetts Bay government by insisting that no civil power could enforce religious injunctions, and by declaring that the colony's land should be purchased from the Indians. He was banished from the colony, ahead of Mrs. Hutchinson, and scrupulously bought a tract of land from the Indians at the head of Narragansett Bay, where he established Providence in 1636. While in London to procure a charter for the new colony of Rhode Island and prevent its being annexed by Massachusetts Bay, he wrote *The Bloudy Tenet, of Persecution, for Cause of Concience* (London, 1644). It was a challenge to Cotton's view by a plea for religious liberty as a natural right, and separation of church and state, adding that political sovereignty rested in the people to whom the rulers were responsible. No one else went that far in toleration and democracy; Quakers and Jews were welcome in Rhode Island.

Cotton replied in a pamphlet, *Wholesome Severity Reconciled with Christian Liberty, or the True Resolution of a Present Controversie Concerning Liberty of Conscience* (London, 1645). Apparently not satisfied, he wrote a much longer work: *The Bloudy Tenent, Washed, and Made White in the Bloud of the Lambe* (London, 1647), discussing restraint of "turbulent and pestilent persons," a problem not yet settled. Williams hit back with *The Bloudy Tenent Yet More Bloody: by Mr. Cottons Endeavour to Wash it White in the Blood of the Lambe* (London, 1652), reviewing the wars undertaken for religious reasons, a sorry record.

Out of this controversy can be sensed the influence of a New World setting on Old World convictions. A lonely voice, Williams wrestled with a new concept: that no church holds copyright on truth, which is more likely to emerge from argument—and argument requires toleration. He himself dropped away from his Baptist church and became a Seeker, accepting no creed. In addition to separate domains for church and state, he initiated religious pluralism, another American characteristic.

Time does not stand still, and the wave of the future washed against the Puritan bastion. A new generation, unacquainted with English repression, was rising. More non-Puritans were arriving. It was a moment for the original founders to reaffirm exactly what they stood for, to distinguish themselves from Separatism on the left, from Presbyterianism on the right, and to exclude Williams's radicalism from their faith and church polity. Yet their hope was more of a memorial than a beacon for the way ahead.

Accordingly, the General Court or assembly of Massachusetts called for a conference of ministers and laymen in late 1646 to frame a statement of beliefs. It was a rigorous undertaking because the founders had never been in complete agreement. They met in Cambridge, soon recessed until the next June, then were interrupted by an epidemic. They met again in September, 1648, and produced a document based on the Reverend Richard Mather's recommendations. When printed locally in 1649, *A Platform of Church Discipline Gathered Out of the Word of God: and Agreed upon by the Elders* . . . became the standard of Congregationalism in New England. Beginning with a clear statement that "Ecclesiastical polity, or church government or discipline is nothing else but that form and order that is to be observed in the church of Christ upon earth," it went on to define a "visible church" and its covenant, enumerate its officers and describe their duties, explain how to engage ministers and teachers, restrict membership, allow united action in temporary synods, and set up new churches as needed.

The Cambridge Platform, however, could not hold the tide from rolling over the Puritan shore. There continued a loosening of authority and an accommodation to pragmatism that became widely noticeable before the end of the century. It was a response to changing cultural and economic patterns in both the New World and the Old. In their opposition the clergy turned into Jeremiahs, lamenting the spiritual decline they perceived.

Perhaps the most prominent bewailers were Increase Mather (1632–1723), son of Richard and husband of John Cotton's daughter, and their son Cotton (1663–1728), whose productive years overlapped his father's at the turn of the century. They were important for output if nothing else: Increase had 130 books and pamphlets published, and Cotton accounted for more than 450! They were respected, learned men whose shining reputations were tarnished by the Salem witchcraft frenzy.

The causes of their gloom were the undeniable decline of Puritan migration to New England and the fall in the ratio of church members to population, the consequent spread of religious toleration, and the new missionary program of an aggressive Church of England in the colonies. Political troubles also contributed to their pessimism. Massachusetts lost its charter due to its intolerance and was reconstituted as a royal colony. The right to vote was extended to male freeholders, not just church members. To the orthodox Puritans the witchcraft fright of 1690 seemed a divine affliction on a sinful people, and the Mathers did not question its reality but encouraged the search for and punishment of Satan's minions.

Increase Mather, inspired by a meeting of ministers who had been stirred by the neglect of religion, published at Boston in 1684 an *Essay for the Recording of Illustrious Providences.* By "providences" he meant examples of God's intervention into human affairs, such as storms, floods, epidemics, earthquakes, the Boston fire, King Philip's War, witchcraft, and diabolical possessions. The book was designed to show God's continuing special interest in New England and His ongoing contest with Satan for New England souls. Though he sought to rout superstition, Mather provided a checklist for delusions on the part of those who agreed that God enjoyed testing His chosen people against Satan's powers. It would bear bitter fruit.

Increase's reputation was such that he was named president of Harvard College, and in 1688 he was sent to London by the Congregational churches to present to the king a petition for restoration of the Massachusetts charter. Failing in this effort, he influenced William III in defining the new government for Massachusetts and in appointing Sir William Phips governor. He returned to Boston in May, 1692, with Phips, who, finding witchcraft flourishing in Salem, appointed a special court to try—and punish—the accused witches. Increase did not object to this procedure.

Engaged by his father's church and preaching steadily during his father's long absence, Cotton Mather, who was vain, arrogant, and pedantic, tried to study witchcraft at first hand by taking into his home a Goodwin girl who was believed to be possessed. She had no trouble imposing on Cotton's credulity, and he confirmed his diagnosis by what he considered to be scientific observations. Accordingly, he published at Boston in 1689 *Memorable Providences Relating to Witchcrafts and Possessions,* which helped set the stage for vigorous accusations of witches. On Governor Phips's arrival, Cotton urged a full investigation by the court.

The immediate cause of the cruelties that followed was the

amazing gullibility of the chief judge, Lieut. Gov. William Stoughton. He believed anything. As guilty verdicts were returned, and innocent, bewildered people were sentenced to be hanged, the Mathers grew uneasy. They led a group of ministers to protest admission of "spectral evidence" (identification of the witch by the bewitched person) in the trials. Increase and Cotton drew up the remonstrance, which was published in 1693 as *Cases of Conscience Concerning Evil Spirits*. This action did not prevent Cotton from attending one public execution and defending it. After Governor Phips halted the proceedings (twenty witches had been hanged) and released all the imprisoned witches, Cotton published *Wonders of the Invisible World* (Boston, 1693), in which he defended the justice of the verdicts in the trials he described. By their stand the Mathers lost face in Boston. Increase gave up the presidency of Harvard, and Cotton, who aspired to the position, was never asked. When Governor Phips left, they likewise lost their political influence.

It is ironic that, in regard to witchcraft, corrective common sense did not overtake these two theological leaders, but emerged instead from a nonintellectual businessman of Boston, Robert Calef. In *More Wonders of the Invisible World*, Calef denounced witchcraft as a fairy tale and blamed Cotton Mather for much of the frenzied suffering. He finished the book in 1697, but no Boston printer would touch it. It was published in London by enemies of the Mathers in 1700, and at last the voice of reason was heard.

Of course, the concerns of the Mathers were not focused exclusively on witchcraft. Increase wrote *A Brief History of the Warr with the Indians* (Boston, 1676) about King Philip's War, and published some notable sermons. Cotton issued sermons and moral tracts and sent to England in 1701 the manuscript of his *Magnalia Christi Americana, or Ecclesiastical History of New England from its First Planting*, which was published in London, 1702. A monumental tome, it is not very readable because of Cotton's heavy style, ornamented by allusions that principally called attention to his learning. Nevertheless, it preserves numerous details about the religious leaders and theological attitudes in New England. It is history related through biographical sketches and suggests that a glorious period had passed away, leaving the author saddened and somewhat alienated from his society. He did better in *The Accomplished Singer* (Boston, 1721), a discussion of which belongs in this volume's chapter on music.

One other commanding figure should be noted as a contrast to the Mathers—the Reverend John Wise (1652–1725), and not only for his brilliant writing. A man of the world and democratically inclined, he remained very much a political as well as spiritual adviser to his people in Ipswich. Indeed, he was an early example of the Age of Reason with his shouts against witchcraft. When the Mathers proposed an association of clergymen who would have veto power over whom a congregation might call for its pastor (contrary to the Cambridge Platform), he helped bury the suggestion. In 1713 he elaborated on his argument in *The Churches' Quarrel Espoused* (published in New York), defending in a learned, sarcastic, and earnest manner the autonomy of each congregation. Four years later he reverted to this theme in *A Vindication of the Government of New England Churches* (Boston, 1717), bolstering it with a deep faith in human equality which he extended to political activity through an appeal to "the Law of Nature."

The Mathers were not wrong in believing that piety was diminishing in each new American generation. One cause was the dryness of their sermons and those of their confreres. They were not only long but appealed only to the intellect. Listeners were informed, but not stirred or aroused. At the same time a few ministers realized they must become more persuasive in the pulpit to attract the unchurched. A reaction was in the making.

It began in New Jersey about 1726 with a crusade to reach nonmembers by vigorous, popular preaching. It spread south and north and to the frontier. It would split churches, inspire the first popular intercolonial movement, and contribute to the distinctiveness of American culture. Religious life of America was permanently changed by the new emphasis. The movement was called the Great Awakening, and many clergymen deplored its lack of dignity, its emotionalism, and its impermanence. If the ultimate appeal was not "You must be born again!" it was cried in similar words, and the techniques of modern revivals may be traced back to the Great Awakening. The new evangelistic style was practiced in the Congregational pulpit of the Reverend Jonathan Edwards at Northampton, Massachusetts, starting in 1734. He specialized in frightening his parishoners into mass confessions and conversions. His most famous sermon was *Sinners in the Hands of an Angry God* (Boston, 1741), a pleasant little homily vividly depicting the tortures awaiting the unregenerate after death. Edwards's *A Treatise Concerning the Religious Affections* (Boston, 1746) was made up of four sermons, delivered from 1737 to 1743, about manifestations of salvation. He insisted that love of God began with an intuitive and direct vision of the beauty of God, which in turn aroused joy and certainty. Edwards's biographer in the *Dictionary of American Biography* was so intent on showing him to be "the first great philosophic intelligence in American history" that he omitted all mention of the 1741 sermon.

The various local revivals were linked together by the first great itinerant evangelist, who was neither American nor mature. George Whitefield, an Englishman and a friend of Charles and John Wesley, the founders of Methodism, was only twenty-four years old when he first visited America in 1738. On a second trip two years later he made a preaching tour through the seaboard colonies. He was more impulsive than rational in his discourses, and felt his inspiration was infallible. Whitefield was no intellectual, and when his sermons appeared in print they lost much of the effect they had when delivered. For he was a gifted speaker of extraordinary voice, dramatic in his performance, his innocent round face an asset. London actor David Garrick once remarked, "I would give a hundred guineas if I could only say 'O!' like Mr.

Whitefield." The young preacher possessed a way of reducing his audiences to personal despondency over their sins and then energizing a surge for divine forgiveness and holy living. Then he took up a fat collection for his orphanage in Georgia.

When he returned in the summer of 1744, Whitefield found some opposition to his style, though not from his large audiences. He revisited America four times more in the next twenty-six years and died here in 1770. His influence was tremendous, cementing the revival to American Protestantism and insuring its cyclical recurrence. Oddly, Whitefield found Biblical justification for slavery and defended it, although he condemned those slaveholders who were cruel to their Negroes. His message that everyone had charge of his own spiritual destiny, contrary to the Puritans' Calvinism, not only militated against a churchly hierarchy but spilled over into politics on the side of faith in democratic exercise. Those convictions strengthened ties across colonial boundaries and stimulated the eventual establishment of colleges to turn out more ministers and missionaries as well as to provide safe havens for youth. Still, Whitefield is better remembered today for the *Journals* of his missionary tours which were published in six parts from 1738.

If the frontier adopted and especially enjoyed revival methods, the Great Awakening ignited a controversy in New England that divided churches into Old Lights and New Lights. Some clergymen found the evangelical style repugnant, as did many parishoners, and resented the money Whitefield took out of town, labeling him a "spiritual pickpocket." Harvard and Yale, which had welcomed Whitefield in 1740, closed their doors to him in 1744. Two prominent clerical voices protested Edwards, Whitefield, and Company. They belonged to Charles Chauncy (1705–1787) and Jonathan Mayhew (1720–1766), the two most influential liberals of their day, both pastors of Boston churches.

Neither Chauncy nor Mayhew believed in predestination, declaring that man's reason enabled him to choose freely between good and evil. They agreed that the goodness of God was irreconcilable with the Calvinistic doctrine of condemnation of many people for original sin and unconditional election to salvation of others; that human reason must "validate" revelation; and that good works would lead to a saving faith. They preached a merciful God rather than a judgmental God. They had no use for emotional reaction to threats of damnation. Chauncy warned his congregation in *Enthusiasm Described and Cautioned Against* (Boston, 1742) and rebuked Whitefield for his censoriousness. In his *Ministers Exhorted and Encouraged to Take Heed to Themselves and to Their Doctrine* (Boston, 1744), Chauncy told his colleagues they should preach a solid doctrine, "not a meer Notion, a Fancy that has existence no where but in their own over-heated brains." Sudden impulses and visions do not emanate from the Holy Spirit, he declared, and enthusiasm easily led to fanaticism. Here he was replying to evangelists who denounced clergymen unless they too had had an emotional experience of regeneration. He was a forerunner of those who eventually called themselves Universalists.

Mayhew was more sensitive to the civil society he lived in. His *Seven Sermons* which he delivered in 1748 were published the next year. They were reprinted in London, 1750. He startled his parishoners by arguing that man had a duty and a natural right to question all religious doctrine. Enlarging on this theme, he published *A Discourse Concerning Unlimited Submission and Non-Resistance to the Higher Powers* (Boston, 1750). Here he stated that in case of civil laws contrary to God's laws, disobedience was justified; and while man should honor and obey a good king if he rules justly, if he turns tyrant they should throw off their allegiance and resist him. This stand was a long, long way down the road from a deferential John Cotton.

Much as the foregoing men might differ in religious outlook, their views all rose from varying interpretations of the Holy Word. Nothing surpassed the Bible as authority. Most of the first settlers had brought with them the Geneva Bible, printed in Geneva, Switzerland, from 1560 on and embodying a translation by Calvinists. It required a new generation to accept the King James Version of 1611, which after the middle of the century superseded the Geneva Bible in popularity.

The first whole Bible to be printed in this country is unintelligible today. It is a translation of the King James Version into the language of the Natick Indians of Massachusetts, a labor of love by the Reverend John Eliot (1604–1690), pastor at Roxbury. The latter also served as missionary to the "Indians of the West" (i.e., about thirty miles west of Boston). Among his converts were twenty-four Indians who became preachers. Since the Naticks had no written language, Eliot, who had learned their tongue orally, used the English alphabet to write down the words as they sounded to him. He first translated the New Testament phonetically and had it printed in Cambridge in 1661. Two years later he completed the translation of the Old Testament, and the two parts were put together in what is called the *Up-Biblum God* (1663), a thick, small quarto. The full title reads *Mamvsee Wunneetu Panatamwe Up-Biblum God Naneesive Nukkone Testament kah Wonk Wusku Testament.* Reading the language presents no insuperable problem: just sound the words as they are spelled.

Who paid for the printing? The Corporation in London for the Propagation of the Gospel. But it could not afford the whole expense, and Eliot paid the balance. There was a further problem. After Eliot distributed this Bible to his charges, it meant nothing to them. They couldn't read it; they had never seen their language in any written form. So poor Eliot had to teach them to read. Evidently he succeeded, because in 1685 it was necessary to reprint this Bible. The tribe was small and in the next century was wiped out or absorbed by other tribes, and the language was lost. Yet this fact does not affect the monetary value of the "Eliot Indian Bible" among collectors. About forty copies are known today. A copy sold at auction in 1966 brought $43,000. Another copy, not in fine condition, sold at the end of 1977 for $25,000.

The first Bible in a European language to be printed here was in German. It was typeset and published at Germantown, Pennsylvania, by Christopher Saur in 1743. His *Biblia das ist: die Heilige Schrift Altes und Neues Testaments* was issued in 1,200 copies. Saur had obtained Fraktur type from the Luther foundry in Frankfort and as his copy text used the Baron Canstein Bible printed at Halle earlier in the century. He also corrected about a hundred misprints in the Halle edition.

Demand widened among the German settlers, and a second edition was printed in 1763; a third edition of 3,000 copies came out in 1776. However, the latter is the scarcest of the three editions because not many copies were bound. Saur was a Loyalist, and in the second year of the Revolution his shop was invaded and most of the printed sheets were carried off by rebel soldiers. They wanted the paper for cartridges and gun wadding.

Why was there no English Bible in the colonies? Thereby hangs a tale. King James appointed a committee of scholars to make a new translation of the Bible, and when they finished their work this version was considered to belong to the king as head of the Church of England. Robert Barker held the king's patent as Royal Printer, and the Bible was his privilege; so he printed the new translation in folio size in black letter for church use in 1611. For individuals he issued in 1613 a quarto-sized volume in roman type. Barker did a poor job of proofreading, and his use of italics was not consistent. On the other hand, he was never furnished with an authentic manuscript, but suffered the supervision of a scholarly committee.

After a few years it was perceived that the so-called King James Version was going to be a profitable item. Cambridge University Press, which by its charter was permitted to publish "all manner of books," boldly brought out a King James Version Bible with corrections in 1629. It reinforced its right to do so by buying a manuscript of some kind of the committee's translation.

Barker had died, and his royal patent was taken over by his partners and lessees, who quarreled. Oxford University Press, which wanted to get into the act, bought the presses and equipment from one of Barker's partners in 1644 and felt it had thereby acquired the right to print the King James Bible. After the middle of the century this preferred Bible was securely in the jealous hands of the two university presses, and temporarily there was no king. Without their permission, any printing of the King James Version was illegal, and they did not grant permission to anyone. So for 165 years Americans had to import their Bibles if they wanted the newest and best version.

With the onset of the American Revolution, however, the importation of books largely ceased. Moreover, at least one printer began to think that the Cambridge-Oxford stranglehold on the King James Version could no longer be enforced in America. Robert Aitken of Philadelphia felt he had been deprived of a best-seller long enough by what was now an alien publisher. In 1777 he brought out the New Testament in the 1611 translation, and he reprinted it in 1778 for the use of schools. His lead was followed by printers in Trenton, Wilmington, Boston, and two others in Philadelphia. Aitken's boldness increased and, in imitation of the English authorized version, he petitioned the Continental Congress, whose *Journals* he printed, to give him authority to print the whole Bible. Meanwhile, he went ahead setting type. Congress finally acted in September 1782 with an authorization and even recommended his Bible to the American public. It is the only time Congress has ever authorized a Bible. Late in 1782 Aitken issued *The Holy Bible, Containing the Old and New Testaments: Newly Translated out of the Original Tongue; and with the Former Translations Diligently Compared and Revised.* Not a word about King James appears on the title page, which is graced instead by the arms of Pennsylvania! It is a small book, little more than 3 by 5½ inches, but with 1,440 pages in fine print.

Aitken pressed out a whopping 10,000 copies. Then peace reopened the book trade with England, and more attractive Bibles appeared in competition. Ten years later Aitken had not made back his costs; in fact he mentioned that he had lost

£4,000 on the book. Yet by 1940 only fifty copies could be located. An Aitken Bible is worth several thousand dollars today.

One more American Bible needs to be mentioned. Noah Webster, the lexicographer, wanted to revise the King James Version by altering words whose meanings had changed since 1611. He had found some 150 words and phrases that were misleading, since usage had shifted. Later revisers of the Bible accepted most of his corrections. He entitled his work *The Holy Bible, Containing the Old and New Testaments, in the Common Version. With Amendments of the Language* (New Haven, 1833). It had a slow sale, but was reprinted in 1841. Webster considered it his most important work and was disappointed by its reception. Today collectors pay little attention to it, making it about a hundred-dollar book.

In their objection to Quakers, the Puritan fathers were right about one thing: if they were going to allow personal revelation as much authority as the Bible, sects would be encouraged, and there was no gainsaying them. Roger Williams's tolerance was dangerous in their view, but eventually it had to be allowed because the majority of new settlers were not of Puritan persuasion. Of interest here are not the new denominations that resulted from cleavages among Baptists, Presbyterians, and Methodists, but new kinds of Christian faith—new in emphasis, theology, organization, and outlook—which sprang up here as original thinkers gained followers and organized new churches. Four may be briefly described from their own published sources: the Shakers, the Mormons, the Millerites, and the Christian Scientists. Each has a considerable literature.

Nine adults from England debarked at New York in August, 1774. They believed they were possessed of an intoxicating secret: among them was the reincarnated Christ! They had belonged to a band in England that relied on the inspiration of the Holy Spirit, expected the imminent return of Christ, and sought to live as they thought the primitive Christians did. What was unique about them was that they believed the God who was both Father and Mother would show him- and herself the second time as a woman. They had no organization and no church but liked to interrupt services in the Church of England. Ann Lees, an illiterate textile worker of Manchester, had been converted to this doctrine in 1758, when she was twenty-two. Four years later she married Abraham Standerin, a blacksmith, and in the course of time gave birth to four children, all of whom died in infancy. Convinced that she was being punished for her sins, she began exhorting others to repent. Her own group exhibited some strange shaking and shuffling in their services that led to speaking in tongues and fervent prayers. Witnesses called them "Shaking Quakers."

In 1773 Ann had been arrested for disturbing an Anglican service. While in jail she had two revelations. One convinced her that the original sin of Adam and Eve was sexual intercourse, and the only way to obtain salvation was to practice celibacy and confess all other sins. Apparently God's creatures were not to procreate themselves. The second vision was more startling: the Second Coming was not a future event; it had already occurred—in her! This was too much for most of her group, especially the couple who had been accepted as leaders. It was also too much for her husband, but he stayed with her. A few months after her release, a loyal follower had a vision of America, and Ann interpreted it as meaning her work should go on there. A wealthy convert paid for passage of the nine.

On the eve of revolution, New York City ignored Ann. Both she and her husband worked to sustain themselves, until two of her followers leased some land up the Hudson, above Albany, and built a log cabin. Ann moved there in the spring of 1776, her repressed and perplexed husband having wandered off, lost to history. Ann started using her maiden name and dropped the s. At Niskeyuna she had further revelations, against the war and against private property. Only a few converts were made. Being English and a pacifist, she was accused of Loyalist sympathy and was arrested in July, 1780. After a few months in jail, she was released by order of

Governor George Clinton and remanded to her brother as bondsman for her good behavior. In the spring of 1781 Mother Ann Lee, as she was called, started on a tour of New England.

Her first converts were from families that had been aroused by some revival and then found regular church affiliation disappointing. They wanted assurance of salvation, and Ann Lee provided it: Christ had returned in her, and to achieve salvation one need only accept that fact. Still, there was no church, and although a few of her followers moved close together, there were no integrated communities. Ann Lee preached and traveled for two years before returning to the locale of her first followers. She died there in 1784.

After her death her converts, believing themselves to be "the first witnesses of the Gospel of Christ's Second Appearing," organized as a church and called themselves the United Society of Believers in Christ's Second Appearing. Their noisy services, their marching and dancing, scandalized their neighbors, who called them Shakers. One convert, a Baptist revivalist preacher named Joseph Meachum, became the acknowledged leader in 1787 and gathered some believers into a celibate community at New Lebanon, New York. He was practical enough to see that it was necessary to cultivate friendly relations with the surrounding area in order for the cooperative community to sell its products and survive. He did much traveling and organized ten other communities in New England, with separate dormitories for men and women.

The first three publications about the Shakers were antagonistic. Valentine Rathbun, a Baptist minister in Pittsfield, Massachusetts, had participated in the worship services of Mother Ann Lee at Niskeyuna, but before being accepted into full membership he dropped out and wrote what he considered to be an exposé—a pamphlet entitled *An Account of the Matter, Form, and Manner of a New and Strange Religion, Taught and Propagated by a Number of Europeans, Living in a Place Called Nisqueunia, in the State of New-York* (Providence, 1781). It was reprinted at Hartford,

Boston, and Norwich in the same year under a different title, beginning *Some Brief Hints of a Religious Scheme*. The tract was savage enough to arouse some mob violence against the Shakers. It was followed the next year by another pamphlet, *A Narrative of the Strange Principles, Conduct and Character of the People Known by the Name of Shakers* (Worcester, 1782), by Amos Taylor, an apostate from the Shaker group at Harvard, Massachusetts. Then Benjamin West, who had joined the Shakers, withdrew because he believed their teachings to be contrary to the Bible. In consequence he published *Scriptural Cautions Against Embracing a Religious Scheme* (Hartford, 1783). He said they were "to labour in their dance to mortify the lusts of the flesh. Hence they use these expressions in their dance: 'Labour, labour, mortification before redemption!'"

Mother Ann Lee did not dictate a reply to any of these. It was Joseph Meachum who finally decided that the inflammatory publications should be answered by something positive and sympathetic. He wrote and published anonymously *A Concise Statement of the Principles of the Only True Church According to the Gospel of the Present Appearance of Christ. As Held to and Practised upon by the Followers of the Living Saviour, of New Lebanon, & c.* (Burlington, 1790).

There was a lull of a decade in expansion and publication. Then, taking advantage of the revivals in the West (the Second Great Awakening) in 1800 and after, the Shakers moved to establish new communities in Ohio, Indiana, and Kentucky and issued various explanatory publications. Emphasis was less on theology and more on the advantages of communitarian living. But the Shakers carried the seeds of their own extinction in celibate living. For a time they offset it by conversions and by adoption of orphans, but the imbalance of age increased. About 1830 they numbered some six thousand members; but in the morning of its youth, America could not believe that such living was the means to settle a continent. The number of Shakers dwindled steadily until only half a dozen aged women survive today in the East.

In 1823, near Manchester in western New York, a farm boy had a different revelation from an angel named Moroni, who informed him of buried records in a nearby hill. He was Joseph Smith, Jr., age seventeen. However, the records were not precisely located or allowed into his hands until 1827, after he was married. What he found on digging were plates which had the appearance of gold, each six by eight inches and covered with unintelligible engravings. The characters resembled Egyptian glyphs, but then he uncovered "two transparent stones" through which he "translated the record by the gift and power of God."

Briefly, the plates revealed that about 600 B.C. a company of Israelites sailed to America. Two nations developed from them that waged war on each other for centuries. Christ also came to America after his resurrection and preached. In A.D. 384 in one last battle only the victorious dark-skinned Lamanites survived, and they became what Columbus called Indians. The last prophet of the defeated Nephites, named Mormon, wrote the history found by Smith, although it was completed by Moroni, son of Mormon. It contained many quotations from the Bible, and the style is similar to the King James Version.

Smith dictated his translation to Oliver Cowdery, a local teacher, over a period of a year or two. The story got out, and Smith began gathering both converts and jealous enemies. The plates were then returned to the custody of the angel Moroni and have never been seen again. In 1829, a contract was made with a printer in Palmyra to print and bind 5,000 copies of the translation for $3,000; the money was furnished by a convert who mortgaged his farm. In Palmyra a weekly periodical was also published called *The Reflector,* whose editor began printing chapters from Smith's book before it was published separately. Initially he was sympathetic with the great discovery but grew increasingly critical of the sect and sarcastic about the "Golden Book Apostle." The people of the region were divided between believing Smith and ridiculing him.

The Book of Mormon, "by Joseph Smith, Junior, Author

and Proprietor," and running to nearly 600 pages, appeared at Palmyra in 1830. A leaf at the end contained an attestation by Cowdery and two other men that they had seen the golden plates, and another statement by eight witnesses to a similar testimony. At this juncture Smith, two of his brothers, Cowdery, and two friends joined together in establishing a church, known as the Church of Jesus Christ of Latter-Day Saints. Five thousand copies of the book seemed like a lot, and indeed the edition satisfied demand for half a dozen years. It was peddled door to door by eager disciples, and members grew increasingly uncomfortable in their location. Smith continued to have revelations and saw a new Zion somewhere in the West. Some of his followers moved to Missouri, and he led others to Kirtland, Ohio, where they built a temple. At Zion (Independence), Missouri, the second great source book of the church was published in 1833: *A Book of Commandments for the Government of the Church of Christ*. It consisted of revelations to Smith dictated again to Cowdery, and sermons, but the book was not completed. After 160 pages were printed, a mob destroyed the press.

A new edition was printed at Kirtland in 1835 under a revised title: *Doctrines and Covenants of the Church of the Latter Day Saints*. One of the additional chapters dealt with marriage and was actually written by Cowdery during Smith's absence. In it he said a wife should have one husband, and a husband one wife. Smith was not happy about the addition, and later it was repudiated because it was not a revelation of Smith's. The church in Kirtland also published the second edition of *The Book of Mormon* in 1837, in another order of 5,000 copies. The book was a little smaller and thicker than the first. This time Joseph Smith, Jr., was labeled translator instead of author.

Continued persecution in Missouri led Smith to call the Mormons eastward to a new Zion on the Mississippi in Illinois which he named Nauvoo. By 1842 this city of 25,000 was the largest in the state. He obtained a charter from the state which permitted the group to be almost self-governing and to have its own militia, under the command of Smith.

There the third edition of *The Book of Mormon* was published in 1840, although it had to be printed and bound in Cincinnati. The *Doctrines and Covenants* was reprinted at Nauvoo in 1844, 1845, and 1846.

Dissension broke out in Nauvoo, and a group opposed to Smith started a newspaper in 1844. Opposition could not be tolerated because, to Smith, it was more than a difference of opinion; it was a theological error and therefore a sin. Smith now made a fatal mistake: he destroyed the noxious printing shop. The state government could not ignore this act, and Smith was put under arrest, even though he was running for president of the United States. He and his brother Hyrum were taken to jail in Carthage, where a lawless, vindictive mob shot them in June, 1844.

There were five contenders to succeed Smith, and the majority of members favored Brigham Young. He decided the group should move beyond the reach of "Gentiles," as the Mormons called all other people. The exodus began in 1846, and after a winter in Iowa, the movers settled near the Great Salt Lake. Those remaining in Illinois and Missouri, objecting to Young and his endorsement of polygamy, formed the Reorganized Church of Jesus Christ of Latter-Day Saints under the leadership of Smith's widow and young son. Its headquarters is in Independence, Missouri.

Four months after the murder of Joseph Smith, more than 50,000 Americans gathered in their churches and homes from New England to the Ohio Valley to greet the returned Christ. The date was Tuesday, October 22, 1844. They were Millerites, followers of William Miller, a former officer in the War of 1812 and a farmer turned prophet. After a two-year study of the Bible, Miller became convinced in 1818 that Christ would return to earth between March 21, 1843, and March 21, 1844. He based his prophecy on a mathematical interpretation of the eighth chapter of the Book of Daniel. Not until 1831 did he feel moved to preach this doctrine, and in the next decade he made a few converts to the advent faith, including several ministers. Miller was not interested in starting a new church, just in preparing people for judgment at the Second Coming.

His prophecy usually required several lectures to explain and justify. He published a summary in 64 pages entitled *Evidence from Scripture & History of the Second Coming of Christ about the Year A.D. 1843, and of His Personal Reign of 1,000 Years* (Brandon, Vermont, 1833). This pamphlet was lengthened to 223 pages when revised under the same title in 1835 and reprinted in 1836 and 1838. Miller was invited to preach in numerous small towns and their churches. A dozen ministers took up his theme and spread his prophecy. Late in 1839 he made a faithful disciple of the Reverend Joshua Himes of Boston, who was a born promoter. Himes wanted to tackle the cities. Early in 1840 he started in Boston a Millerite paper, *Signs of the Times,* which began as a semimonthly and became a weekly in 1842. At the same time Himes opened a Second Advent library of various pamphlets which converts could buy and distribute to others.

The first Millerite camp meeting took place in New Hampshire in the summer of 1842 and attracted ten to fifteen thousand persons. Three hundred copies of an illustrated prophetic chart—an extremely rare item today—were distributed. Himes compiled a hymn book, *The Millenial Harp* (Boston, 1842), for the next several camp meetings to be held in a huge tent he ordered for that purpose. In November, 1842, he started a daily in New York City called *The Midnight Cry.* After a month it became a weekly. This paper and *Signs of the Times* are reliable sources on the movement.

As the first date of Miller's prophecy approached, a comet appeared in the sky late in February. Since it had not been forecast, it seemed to be a portent. The "last year" rolled in with some anxiety for the Millerites, but no panic or delirium. The year ran out, and nothing happened beyond the jeers of the unbelievers. Miller confessed his disappointment and admitted there must be some error in his calculations. Then one of his disciples, Samuel Snow, refigured the prophecy and came up with a new and exact terminal date: Tuesday, October 22, 1844. It aroused the faithful to new expectation. Neither Miller nor Himes accepted the date until early October.

With a definite judgment day in prospect, some strange things began to happen among the more than 50,000 Millerites. Some farmers did not bother to gather their harvest, and those who did saw no point in fall planting. A few of the faithful sold their houses and closed their stores. Stolen goods were returned and crimes were confessed as the frightened tried to cleanse their souls. No ascension robes were made or sold; that is a persistent fiction. There were no gatherings on hilltops; only a group of about 150 hiked out of Philadelphia on October 21 and camped in a field. The vast majority met in their homes or churches, and waited and prayed.

When nothing happened on October 22, both Millerite papers confessed to being twice disappointed, but insisted the great day was not far off and urged patience and confident expectation. A general conference was held in April, 1845, to hold the deflated movement together. Miller, his health broken, bowed off stage with a last pamphlet, *Apology and Defence* (Boston, 1845). He died in 1849 in his sixty-eighth year. His views never squared with the enormous interest at this very time in foreign missions, based on a faith that the Second Coming would not occur until all the heathen had heard the saving word of Christ.

A few Millerite ministers were led by Hiram Edson to a different interpretation of Daniel's prophecy, which concluded that man would never know the exact date of the Second Coming. They added a doctrine that Saturday was the true Sabbath. In 1855 the headquarters of the group was moved to Battle Creek, Michigan, and the name Seventh-Day Adventists was adopted in 1860. It is now a separate denomination.

Coming to maturity as the religiously agitated 1840s began was a farm girl of New Hampshire named Mary Baker. She was subject to hysterical seizures, went to school only intermittently, but read widely on spiritual questions. At the end of 1843, when she was twenty-two, she married and was

64

widowed a few months later, before her son was born. Thereafter she lived listlessly with relatives and tried teaching, but was plagued by ill health. She married a dentist in 1853 and lived quietly if not happily. Twice during the Civil War she consulted "Doctor" Phineas Quimby, a faith healer in Maine who was studying to learn the secret of his success. He put her on the road to health. She read his writings and also began studying the healing power of Jesus as recounted in the four Gospels.

In 1866 she separated from her husband and exercised some healing influence among Spiritualistic friends in Lynn, Massachusetts. A new faith began formulating in her mind, and she started writing a book and teaching students her methods. As she developed her principles she had difficulty explaining her system because she used metaphysical terms, knew little about anatomy, and had never mastered English grammar and usage. The ultimate product was *Science and Health with Key to the Scriptures,* published at Boston in 1875 in 1,000 copies. She had taken back the name of her first husband and listed herself as Mary Baker Glover on the title page.

In the book she asserted that "Spirit is God, and man is his image and likeness. Therefore, man is not material; he is spiritual." Again, "Spirit is immortal Truth; matter is mortal error." The five senses report not matter, but beliefs of the mortal mind. The salvation of mankind is to be found in conquering the temporal and unreal—namely, disease, evil, and death. Since no evil comes from God, "the basis of all disease is error or belief; destroy the belief and the sick will recover."

Some of Mrs. Glover's students in Lynn formed a Christian Scientists' Association in 1876 and secured a charter in 1879 as "The Church of Christ, Scientist." They met in houses. Meanwhile, Mrs. Glover was married a third time, to Asa Eddy. Eventually several members withdrew, protesting Mrs. Eddy's frequent litigation and displays of temper. In 1882 she moved to Boston, where her husband died of heart trouble (she called in a physician), although Mrs. Eddy termed it "mesmeric poisoning" by an enemy. In Boston she operated a Metaphysical College whose graduates became missionary practitioners of Christian Science. Her church had no pastor; services were conducted by two readers, one using the Bible, the other reading a commentary from *Science and Health*. Everything was managed according to the *Church Manual* Mrs. Eddy wrote and continually revised.

She had revised *Science and Health* in 1878 by taking the first two chapters from the first edition and adding three new chapters. It was printed in only 200 copies. Either of the first two editions is difficult to find today. The third edition, 1881, contained an interesting reference to "malicious animal magnetism," by which she explained that evil-minded persons could affect others with disease or misfortune. Since she believed the mind was all-powerful, it was not inconsistent with her doctrine. The book was selling widely to the growing number of converts. For the sixteenth edition of 1886 she sought the help of a literary adviser. He improved her style and even rewrote some sections, so that the book read much better.

Mrs. Eddy went into semiretirement in 1889 by moving to Concord, New Hampshire, although she kept a firm hand on the Mother Church in Boston. In the 1905 edition of *Science and Health* (which she also constantly revised) she stated that drugs might be used to relieve excessive pain. During her last illness, probably gallstones, she was treated with morphine. In 1908 she was carried back to a house in Boston, where she died in 1910. Her estate was appraised at more than $2.5 million. Her interpretation of Jesus in her book remains the foundation of the church she founded. No one would have been more astounded by her wealth and her doctrine than the Puritan founders of the city where she flourished.

The foregoing titles represent some of the sources historians must examine in determining how religious earlier Americans were and how they expressed their religious feelings. Historian William McLoughlin insists that Americans are committed to religion in ways that Europeans are not. Our acceptance of religious pluralism, he says, has not broken down our concept of what being religious means—which only a saint could measure up to. Our "denunciation of American materialism, huckstering, and lusting for the 'Almighty Dollar' . . . is a testimony to our commitment to religion. And even our dreams of success—in terms of higher standards of living and the mass distribution of 'creature comforts'—can be described better as a variant upon the search for a new Eden or the coming of the Kingdom of God on earth as we think it is in heaven."

CHAPTER FOUR

Budding American Literature

Scene from Tyler's The Contrast,
as first published in 1790

CHAPTER FOUR

Budding American Literature

F THERE WAS an American Renaissance in literature, it spread over the middle third of the nineteenth century, when such authors as Poe, Emerson, Longfellow, Hawthorne, Holmes, Whittier, Melville, Lowell, Thoreau, Stowe, and Whitman were active. They were immediately preceded by Irving, Bryant, and Cooper. Literary collectors usually confine themselves to those big names or to much more recent authors. But, before all this blossoming, what were the roots of American literature?

The literary historian finds he must strike a balance between the patriots who attach undiscriminating importance to all American authors, and the pretentious modern critics who believe that, outside of Melville and Whitman, America had no literature until the advent of O'Neill, Hemingway, and Faulkner in this century. Both views blur what happened. American literature began in a European culture imported to a new continent, where it was transformed by new conditions of living and higher expectations into different values. The new literature reflected both nostalgia and buoyant self-assertion.

Even though English literature may still set the standards for comparison, it is as wrong to say there were no American authors worth noting until 1830 or 1920, as it is to elevate the beginners of the 1600s and 1700s above their modest accomplishments. There is an American tradition in letters which collectors perceived before some modern critics did. The rediscovery of the writers identified in this chapter has produced a more informed and discriminating judgment of the rise of American literature.

Few of their works "made in America" can be read today with unqualified pleasure and admiration. The exigencies of making a living in the wilderness or in rude towns absorbed most talents. Art requires some leisure. Besides, the ready availability of books from England allowed Americans to enjoy them without laboring to produce them. The first aim, to create a national literature celebrating republican virtues and grandiose landscapes, was not only chauvinistic but misleading. The parade of national virtues is not what endures; it is the universality of human values and emotions that characterizes great literature.

Consider the first poets. Anne Dudley Bradstreet was born in England about 1612, the daughter of Puritan Thomas Dudley. Her father migrated to Massachusetts in 1630 as deputy governor under John Winthrop, whom he succeeded four years later. Anne was well schooled and read widely. She was married in 1628 to Simon Bradstreet, by whom she had eight children. They crossed the Atlantic with her family because Simon had been named secretary of the new colony. Anne was a close observer of nature and meditated about the meaning of life. Happy in her marriage, her reflections loosened the bonds of strict Calvinism, and she began to write poems. Some of them were sermons in verse, but a few communicated deeply felt experiences, simply and warmly expressed. Her models were Spenser and Sidney and the Huguenot poet du Bartas. By 1650 there were enough poems to make a book, and they were taken back to England by her brother-in-law. There they were published anonymously that year without her knowledge, under the title of *The Tenth Muse Lately Sprung Up in America,* the book running to more than 200 pages. It was reprinted with some revisions at

Boston in 1678 and 1758. Anne, who died in 1672, could join the company of minor English poets of the day.

More famous, but a worse poet, was the Reverend Michael Wigglesworth (1631–1705). He was brought to Massachusetts as a boy, graduated from Harvard in 1651, and occupied the church at Malden for the rest of his life. In frightening terms he described the Judgment Day in a rythmic ballad measure, familiar to his readers, and called it *The Day of Doom*. It was apparently first published at Cambridge in 1662 or 1663, and 1,800 copies were sold in the first year. The region obviously had an appetite for such gloomy fare. No copies of the first edition or a perfect copy of the second survive. The oldest known survivor is the one printed in London (1666). The poem was republished in Boston and in England frequently, reaching ten editions by 1777 and five more thereafter. It attains occasional flights of poetic expression, but it remains Puritan theology in verse. The poet succeeded, unconsciously, in sketching a God of repulsive character. Now the poem is read as a curiosity. Wigglesworth also wrote two other didactic works of lesser success.

Now regarded as our best early poet is the Reverend Edward Taylor (ca. 1644–1729), but his work was not published until the present century.

Possibly the best of the later published poets was Philip Freneau (1752–1832), who graduated from Princeton in 1771 with James Madison. He was determined to be a poet and sing of America; he showed potential talent, but the Revolution interrupted his literary ambition. He served in arms and was a prisoner of war, an experience that embittered him toward everything British. Then, as editor of a Philadelphia newspaper, he derided every imitation of England he perceived as well as every shortcoming of his fellows. Lacking both tolerance and humor, Freneau was a fine satirist. Suddenly, in 1785, he quit his newspaper and became a coastal sea captain, though he continued to turn out popular verse on simple themes. In 1791 he was employed as a clerk in the State Department by Thomas Jefferson, who encouraged him to start another newspaper as a crusading editor, with Washington and Hamilton as his targets. With Jefferson's election to the Presidency in 1800, Freneau retired again and resumed his poetry. A radical original, he antagonized many people and developed no following. Aside from separate printings of a couple of poems before the war, his first collection, *The Poems of Philip Freneau,* appeared at Philadelphia in 1786. It contained at least two very good poems: "The Wild Honey Suckle" and "The Indian Burying Ground." This collection was revised and expanded into *Poems Written Between the Years 1768 & 1794,* which Freneau himself printed in Monmouth, New Jersey, in 1795. If he was largely forgotten before he died, his reputation has risen somewhat since the middle of this century.

Freneau's contemporary, John Trumbull (1750–1831), attempted a modern epic poem in *M'Fingal* (Philadelphia, 1775, issued in January, 1776). It started as a burlesque of a proclamation issued by British Gen. Thomas Gage at Boston after hostilities began. M'Fingal was a Tory whose fortunes declined as British military efforts failed. After the war, Trumbull rewrote his epic, making it longer, with a strong patriotic climax, and it was printed at Hartford in 1782. A succession of thirty editions followed.

Trumbull's friend Joel Barlow (1754–1812) was a lawyer and army chaplain who celebrated the new nationalism after the Revolution. He considered himself a better poet than he was, and, like *M'Fingal,* his chief work appeared in two versions. He first composed *The Vision of Columbus* (Hartford, 1787) as a patriotic poem of America's discovery and future prospects. It had some popular appeal, going through three editions, which led Barlow to revise and lengthen it under a new title: *The Columbiad* (Philadelphia, 1807). It was no better, just more tedious.

The late eighteenth century was a difficult period for poets. The classical tradition was dying, but romanticism was suspect and slow in emerging. Consequently, taste was confused; what should be admired was uncertain. Time has dated the poets, whose sights were not set high enough; they are seldom read. That is less true of the prose writers.

Mary White Rowlandson started what became a new genre in American letters: the Indian-captivity narrative. She was born about 1640; her death date is not known. She married the Reverend Joseph Rowlandson and had three children. In 1675 they were living thirty-five miles west of Boston in Lancaster, where he was the pastor. Late in the year Chief Metacomet, or King Philip as he had been baptized, aroused his Wapanoags and two neighboring tribes to make war on the growing New England settlements. In the cold dawn of February 10, 1676, the Indians struck the town of Lancaster. After two hours of bloody battle, the Rowlandson house, a stronghold containing thirty-seven persons, was set afire. Twelve inhabitants were killed, one made his escape, and twenty-four were taken prisoner. They were marched away in the snow and were given nothing to eat until the third day. Mary's baby died. For the next several weeks the prisoners were moved from camp to camp up into New Hampshire and Vermont. Eventually the Indians turned south again and sought a ransom for Mary. A representative from Boston went out to the Indian camp and paid the ransom in cloth and cash, and Mary was released on May 3. She was reunited with her husband, but their two surviving children could not be obtained until the end of June. "Thus hath the Lord brought me and mine out of that horrible pit, and hath set us in the midst of Tender-hearted and compassionate Christians," Mary wrote.

What had sustained her throughout her torturous ordeal was her faith. For Mary Rowlandson believed that the Lord had permitted her capture and suffering in order to test her. In that spirit she wrote a testimonial of her experience for her children, but did not allow it to be published in her lifetime. The first edition appeared at Boston in 1682 "at the earnest desire of some friends." No copy survives. A second edition, corrected and amended, was printed at Cambridge the same year. Four copies are known. The title begins: *The Sovereignty and Goodness of God, Together, with the Faithfulness of His Promises Displayed; Being a Narrative of the Captivity and Restauration of Mrs. Mary Rowlandson*. The pamphlet found favor in England and was reprinted in London, also in 1682; that is now the earliest procurable edition. It is known in at least eighteen copies. The copy in the Streeter auction sale of 1967 brought $3,250. Some thirty editions are known, the last published in 1930. It has been called "one of the most widely read pieces of seventeenth-century prose." Mary's familiarity with the Old Testament shows in her own thunderous and flowing style, so reminiscent of that Scripture.

There were later captivity narratives down to the 1890s, and they always found an audience. Some were testimonials to Christian faith, some had political overtones about the perfidy of the French allies of the Indians, some exhibited racial prejudice, some were adventure or horror stories, and a few were fiction, as the genre proved irresistible to hack writers.

The many-sided genius of Benjamin Franklin (1706–1790) included a facet of literary achievement. In an age when style was often ornamented or turgid, he wrote simply, clearly, and flowingly. With his sharp observation of human foibles, his mature and sometimes satiric judgments, and his great humor he was eminently readable then and now, whether explaining practical matters, advising conduct, or giving full rein to his imagination. The first part of his autobiography, carrying his life to 1730, was first published in French as *Mémoires de la Vie Privée* (Paris, 1791). It was translated into English and printed in London (1793) and New York (1794). Another segment was found among Franklin's manuscripts that carried the autobiography to 1757, and it appeared in 1850. For the years 1774, 1775, and 1782, Franklin wrote about his role as diplomatic negotiator, intending to incorporate these excerpts into his life story as soon as he reached that period in his narrative, which he never did. It was not difficult, however, for editors to fill in the missing years of autobiography from letters and essays, so that a fairly complete life history in Franklin's words is available. Indeed, it stands almost as a textbook on how to write an autobiography.

His essays on a hundred different subjects are still delightful today. His *Almanacks* from 1733 to 1758 are full of wisdom in anecdotes, maxims, and proverbs attributed to Poor Richard Saunders. They sold 10,000 copies annually. During his long voyage to England in 1757 Franklin summed up Poor Richard's counsels on economy and thrift in a speech attributed to Father Abraham, an old man at an auction. Franklin's nephew in Boston published the piece separately from the 1758 almanac as *Father Abraham's Speech*. Later editions were entitled *The Way to Wealth*. By 1900 it had been reprinted at least 400 times in sixteen languages. As Carl Van Doren wrote, "it long ago passed from literature into the general human speech."

Franklin was the first American to be recognized abroad as a scientist, philosopher, and diplomat. He is continually rediscovered and read today, his wit imperishable, his easy style appealing, and his wisdom still on target and useful. Above all else he demonstrated an American way of thinking. Not surprisingly, twenty thousand persons attended his funeral in Philadelphia. A few collectors have devoted themselves to Franklin's writings and imprints, although he offers such a rich table of viands that they sometimes must select the particular dishes they wish to consume.

The colonial theater got off to an early start. The first was opened in Williamsburg in 1716; the second in Charleston in 1735; then in Philadelphia in 1749, and New York in 1750. These theaters offered contemporary comedies and Shakespearean plays by traveling troupes from England. American playwrights were slow in appearing before the nineteenth century.

Thomas Godfrey (1736–1763) started as a poet, but before his early death turned out a tragedy, "The Prince of Parthia." It was not printed until 1765 in Philadelphia in *Juvenile Poems on Various Subjects . . . by the Late Mr. Thomas Godfrey, Junr.* The play carries the distinction of being the first written by an American to be performed, or at least announced as scheduled for performance, at Philadelphia in 1767. No report on the production has been found. It had an

Oriental setting, and after violent actions and dark passions, both heroine and hero commit suicide. It is not altogether a bad play, but Godfrey did not live to develop his talent.

A later playwright did much better. He wrote the first native comedy to be enacted here, and it is still revived from time to time. The unlikely author was Royall Tyler (1757–1826), born in Boston, which frowned upon the stage. During the Revolution he served on the staff of Gen. Benjamin Lincoln. After studying in the office of John Adams, he practiced law in Vermont and became chief justice of the state supreme court. Yet his interest in literature was constant, and he wrote several dramas and romances. His greatest success was *The Contrast,* a comedy in five acts, performed in New York in 1787. It shows the influence of Richard Brinsley Sheridan. The "contrast" was between an amoral English fop pursuing an innocent American girl, and a sturdy, honest American who saves her and wins her hand. A particularly popular character was introduced in Jonathan, a comic Yankee rustic who became a stage type. He was the original of the expression "Brother Jonathan" (for an American) as distinguished from "John Bull" (a typical Englishman). The play was not printed until 1790, in Philadelphia, and President Washington was one of the subscribers. It was illustrated with a scene from the stage production.

The other playwright now remembered is William Dunlap (1766–1839), virtually the founder of American drama. While growing up in New York he attended theatrical performances by British officers stationed there in 1777–81 and studied painting. After the war he went to London as a pupil of Benjamin West, the American artist who attained such fame in England. Dunlap spent more time indulging his love of the theater in London and saw plays by Shakespeare and Sheridan. When he returned to New York in 1787, he tried his hand at writing a comedy, which was never played or published. But two years later he came to notice with another comedy, *The Father, or American Shandyism* (New York, 1789). Its success brought him out of the studio and into the theater, as author, director, and producer. He offered a new play annually.

The Fatal Deception, or the Progress of Guilt, played in 1794, was a kind of romantic tragedy. It was not printed until 1806, when it appeared under the title of *Leicester. The Archers, or Mountaineers of Switzerland* (New York, 1796) was an opera in three acts. It was followed by *Tell Truth and Shame the Devil* (New York, 1797), a comedy based on a French play. Possibly his best play was a historical drama, *André* (New York, 1798). It has appeared in modern anthologies. Dunlap became director and manager of New York's Park Theatre. He turned to translating and staging French and German plays, but could not make a profit. In 1805 he declared himself bankrupt, but the next year was rehired by the owner of the Park Theatre and stayed five years. Then he returned to painting and held a state office for two years. As a struggling artist he helped found the National Academy of Design in 1826. Clearly Dunlap was more versatile than truly talented; if he was a competent playwright, he was not original. He is better remembered as an art historian for two books: *History of the American Theatre* (New York, 1832) and *History of the Rise and Progress of the Arts of Design in the United States* (New York, 1834; two volumes).

In his bibliography *American Fiction* (Huntington Library, 1969), Lyle H. Wright lists less than forty titles of fiction printed before 1800. Our first novelists adopted the epistolary form with which the English novel began. The first was William Hill Brown (1765–1793). Had he lived longer he might have developed as a writer, but his first novel, *The Power of Sympathy: or, the Triumph of Nature. Founded in Truth* (Boston, 1789) has little literary merit. Through a series of letters, the plot focuses on a young man who shoots himself when he discovers that his sweetheart is actually his half sister. By emphasizing the "truth" of the tales they had to tell, the early novelists sought to overcome public objection to fiction. The melodrama was published anonymously by

Isaiah Thomas, who did not hesitate to advertise the book as "the first American novel." It was reprinted as late as 1937. There were earlier examples of American fiction, but they were so short as hardly to qualify as novels. Brown wrote one other novel, but it was not published until long after his death.

For years Brown's first novel was attributed to Sarah Wentworth Morton, a Boston writer, because it dealt with a scandal similar to one in her family involving her husband and her sister—a dubious reason, for why should she want to air it? In this century the author has been declared to be Brown, a neighbor of the Mortons.

A much more popular and prolific author was an English actress who settled permanently in America. Susanna Rowson (1762–1824) lived here as a girl for nine years before the Revolution. She returned with her husband in 1793 to fill a three-year contract with the Philadelphia theater. Afterward she went to live in Boston. Obviously talented, she published eight novels, a volume of poetry, and a farce. Mrs. Rowson had published a novel (not her first) in London in 1791 called *Charlotte, a Tale of Truth.* It avoided the letter form and directly told the romantic story of an English girl lured to America with the promise of marriage, but abandoned in New York, where she died in childbirth. It, too, was based on the allegedly true story of one Charlotte Stanley and Capt. John Montresor, and the girl is said to lie buried in Trinity churchyard, New York, under a "not too authentic" tombstone labeled "Charlotte Temple." The book sold 20,000 copies in three years.

When the novel was reprinted in Philadelphia in 1794, it was retitled *Charlotte Temple,* and so it became known in this country. By 1905 the touching story had gone through more than 160 editions! In the 1850s its immense popularity was finally surpassed only by *Uncle Tom's Cabin,* but as late as 1875 a door-to-door salesman could still earn a living from selling *Charlotte Temple* and one other novel. Mrs. Rowson wrote simply and clearly, without much imagination. Actually, she was a realist before that term was used.

It is somewhat mysterious why a similar novel of a heroine in distress, who also suffered a faithless lover and died in childbirth, did not achieve equal popularity. Perhaps it was because it was related in letters. Hannah Webster Foster (1759–1840), a Boston woman and wife of a minister, wrote *The Coquette; or the History of Eliza Wharton; a Novel; Founded on Fact* (Boston, 1797). It contained a moral lesson, of course, and was received well enough to be reprinted annually until 1833, when its sales tapered off. Mrs. Foster never attempted another novel.

The first American to make writing his profession was Charles Brockden Brown (1771–1810). He was a Quaker of Philadelphia. His industry during a short life made him a major novelist, albeit not a great one, who was recognized in England. Brown readily illustrates the complaint of French observer Alexis de Toqueville thirty years later that American authors (Franklin excepted) used an inflated style and pompous imagination to differentiate "literature" from the clear, plain language used in business letters and neighborly conversation.

Brown's first published work was not a novel but a bold essay: *Alcuin: a Dialogue on the Rights of Women* (New York, 1798). Then came four novels in rapid succession: *Wieland* (New York, 1798), and perhaps his best; *Ormond* (New York, 1799) and *Arthur Merwyn* (Philadelphia, 1799–1800), Gothic romances of villainy; and *Edgar Huntley; or, Memoirs of a Sleep Walker* (Philadelphia, 1799) in three volumes, the first novel to use an Indian captivity as its theme. After a short interval he produced two novels of marriage: *Clara Howard* and *Jane Talbot* (both Philadelphia, 1801). He also translated a French work, edited a magazine, and wrote political tracts. In fact, Brown dissipated his energies and did not concentrate on developing his narrative powers. He was a reformer at heart, without a focus. William Dunlap wrote a biography of him. His books do not command premium prices today among collectors.

One other novelist of this time deserves to be mentioned. Hugh Henry Brackenridge (1748–1816) was a classmate of

Philip Freneau and James Madison at Princeton. Early in the Revolution he wrote two plays in blank verse dealing with the war. They were printed but not produced, unless perhaps by students at the Maryland academy he headed. Brackenridge tried several occupations before taking up law and moving to Pittsburgh; like Royall Tyler, he became a justice of the state supreme court. Brackenridge wrote only one novel, but it runs as long as four or five ordinary novels, and its six volumes were produced over a dozen years. *Modern Chivalry: Containing the Adventures of Captain John Farrago, and Teague O'Regan, His Servant* is the first important American fiction to deal with the frontier and to satirize its politics. It is a picaresque novel. If the two main characters sound like Don Quixote and Sancho Panza, that is intentional. Their adventures are inglorious and comic, Teague being extricated by his master from situations beyond his capacity to handle. The author uses Teague to personify the weakness of democracy. He also exposes corruption in high places as the twin evil. "The great moral of this book," he said, "is the evil of men seeking office for which they are not qualified." He was as much an instructor as the lady novelists, but not through pity or sentimentality.

The work bears curious imprints. The first two volumes appeared in Philadelphia in 1792, the third at Pittsburgh in 1793, and the fourth at Philadelphia in 1797. They constitute Part I. After an interval Part II appeared: volume one at Carlisle in 1804, and volume two at Carlisle in 1805. A final part came out in 1815.

No literary critic or literary historian (Van Wyck Brooks excepted) deigns to mention Parson Weems. Yet Mason Locke Weems (1759–1825) was our first native best-selling author. He may have cut a comic figure, but he was a serious, calculating author and a real professional. He was also a sometime Episcopal minister, a fiddler, and a successful itinerant bookseller in the South. Working for Philadelphia publisher Matthew Carey, he dubbed himself a "ragged Mother Carey's chicken." Born in Maryland, he had been well educated abroad, yet he moved easily among poor people as well as plantation owners and city merchants. He could and did sell all kinds of books: novels, plays, poetry, travel accounts, natural history, Bibles, biographies, sermons, and almanacs. Weems sold Rowson's *Charlotte Temple* and Brown's *Wieland* and *Ormond* by the wagonload. In this extrovert, Carey had a superb salesman combined with an author who knew what the public, at least in the South, wanted.

Weems wrote four short biographies of Washington, Franklin, Francis Marion, and William Penn. *The Life and Memorable Actions of George Washington, General and Commander of the Armies of America,* published anonymously, is so little known in first edition that the date was not certain until recently. Written right after Washington's death, it was printed first in Philadelphia by George Keatinge in 1800, then reprinted the same year in Philadelphia in Georgetown, and in Baltimore. The book represented a new genre: the fictionalized biography. It was filled with anecdote, dialogue, and homely scenes. For a time it was second in sales to *Charlotte Temple.* More than seventy editions, including five in German, were published. Collectors who give up trying to find a first are glad to have a fifth edition (1806), because it contains the first appearance of the cherry tree story. Had Weems just heard of it, or did he make it up?

Interspersed among the biographies were half a dozen moral tracts Weems wrote that made him feel he was carrying on his ministry from a moveable pulpit. *God's Revenge Against Murder* (Philadelphia, 1807) was a vivid and powerful diatribe on the sin and punishment of murderers. It was followed by similar titles against gambling, drunkenness, adultery, and duelling. His humor sparkled in several almanacs he prepared. His name became a household word throughout the South from his thirty-one years of traveling. In a day of limited entertainment, he knew how to captivate the reading public.

In competition with Bunyan, Shakespeare, Fielding, Sterne, Smollett, Sheridan, Goldsmith, Johnson, Burns, Byron, Keats, and Shelley, our earliest writers seem hardly to play in the same league. The British authors were readily available here, too. Yet a rising patriotism heartened American writers, and with a few showing the way, later talents were encouraged. In only a few years Washington Irving and James Fenimore Cooper were being eagerly read in Europe as well as here. The American literary bloom blossomed rapidly.

More than in nonfiction, collectors of poetry, drama, and fiction emphasize distinctions of scarcity which have nothing to do with content and tend to be superficial, such as typographical errors, press defects, differences in paper, binding, or trim size. For all that, collectors have been a strong force—along with Professor Moses Coit Tyler of Michigan and Cornell in his critical work of 1878—in directing the attention of academic literary scholars to American writers before the nineteenth century.

CHAPTER FIVE

Contributions to Science

Hydrangea Quercifolia

The familiar hydrangea from Bartram's Travels, *1791*

CHAPTER FIVE

Contributions to Science

ENJAMIN FRANKLIN is remembered as a genial, wise, and witty philosopher-journalist and astute diplomat, in all a sophisticated citizen of the world; but that is not how Europe first knew him. He was seen from abroad as a remarkable colonial scientist. What impressed the Royal Society of London (which gave him its gold medal and elected him to membership) were his two stoves, his speculations in meteorology, his experiments in electricity, his guess that light came from the sun in waves, his lightning rods, his bifocal spectacles, his clock, his marking of the Gulf Stream in the Atlantic. For these achievements St. Andrews and Oxford universities awarded him honorary degrees.

In *An Account of the New Invented Pennsylvanian Fire-Places* (Philadelphia, 1744) Franklin modestly did not proclaim himself inventor of the stove that would bear his name. He did not patent it, and in 1740 he allowed a friend to manufacture and sell it. The pamphlet was an effort to broaden the market. Something over twenty copies survive. (Modern so-called Franklin stoves have eliminated the distinctive feature of the original.) In his several years of electrical experiments Franklin demonstrated and named positive and negative charges, invented a condenser, applied such terms as armature and conductor, and surmised that lighting was electricity. The latter he proved by flying a kite in a summer storm. After he described his experiments to his English friend, Peter Collinson, the latter published for him *Experiments and Observations on Electricity, Made at Philadelphia, in America* (London, 1751). It was enlarged in 1753, and Franklin revised the fourth edition in 1769. The work was translated into French and printed at Paris in 1773. *How to Secure Houses, etc. from Lightning* appeared in *Poor Richard's Almanack* for 1753. While resident in London in 1771, Franklin invented another stove, but it was not publicized until after the war when he returned from Paris. The title was *Description of a New Stove for Burning Pitcoal and Consuming All its Smoke,* and it appeared in the *Transactions* of the American Philosophical Society in 1786. All of Franklin's scientific writings did not get into print, but the remainder are preserved in his letters.

Franklin was always the pragmatist, trying to turn his discoveries and inventions to popular use and benefit. Speaking of his experiments with electricity, the eminent English chemist, Sir Humphry Davy, said: "He has endeavoured to remove all mystery and obscurity from the subject; he has written equally for the uninitiated and for the philosopher; and he has rendered his details amusing as well as perspicuous, elegant as well as simple."

If Franklin was our most famous scientist of colonial times, he was not our only one. I shall not discuss those European scientists who came over here to pursue investigations and returned home to live. My selection is from among our native scientists or those who migrated here and remained, so that we may call their work American contributions to science. Contemporary with Franklin were Cadwallader Colden (1688–1776) of New York, John Winthrop (1714–1779) of Massachusetts, and Jared Eliot (1685–1763) of Connecticut.

Colden, a physician who became a politician, took time to study Newton's principles and to write a critique entitled *An Explication of the First Causes of Action in Matter, and, of the Cause of Gravitation* (New York, 1745). It was printed in

London the next year, and in German at Leipzig in 1751. In that year Colden revised it to appear in London again as *The Principles of Action in Matter*. He mastered the Linnaean system of classifying flora and, with his daughter, catalogued all the plants he could find around his home in Orange County, New York. He sent their study to Linnaeus himself, and the Swedish botanist published it in the Acts of the Royal Scientific Society of Uppsala in 1749. Colden also wrote on medical topics and has been credited with inventing the printing process of sterotyping, though others probably preceded him.

Winthrop was professor of mathematics and physics at Harvard, but his main interest was astronomy. He first came to public notice in 1755 when he published *A Lecture on Earthquakes* in Boston. It was an effort to explain the nature of the upheaval in New England that year, and it appeared while a number of ministers were ascribing the quake to divine wrath. Four years later he published *Two Lectures on Comets* (Boston, 1759), which included the first predicted return of Halley's comet in 1682. Winthrop organized the first scientific expedition in America, and the first sponsored by a college, for the purpose indicated in his report: *Relations of a Voyage from Boston to Newfoundland, for the Observation of the Transit of Venus, June 6, 1761* (Boston, 1761). He supplied the only figures from America on the transit made available to science. He also wrote *Two Lectures on the Parallax and Distance of the Sun* (Boston, 1769). Some of these works and his several astronomical papers were published in the *Philosophical Transactions* of the Royal Society, giving him recognition in England. He was elected to membership in 1766, and the University of Edinburgh gave him an honorary degree.

Eliot was a Connecticut clergyman and physician, and a graduate of Yale. He became prosperous enough to own several farms on which he conducted experiments. Between 1748 and 1759 he published six essays; they are regarded as the most widely read agricultural papers in America. They were gathered into a volume, *Essays Upon Field-Husbandry in New England, as It is or May be Ordered* (Boston, 1760). It is the first American book devoted entirely to agriculture. Eliot later made iron from black sea sand and wrote an explanation of it in 1762. For this he was awarded a gold medal by the Royal Society. (The earliest advice on gardening, however, is found in *The Husbandman's Guide* [Boston, 1710], known in but one copy. It merited a second edition two years later, of which two copies survive. The book contains "monthly directions for planting and sowing" and "excellent receipts for diseases in cattle" plus nonagricultural material. The author has not been identified, and he hardly qualifies as a scientist.)

Nathaniel Bowditch (1773–1838) is all the more remarkable as a scientist because he was entirely self-educated. In the process he read all four volumes of Chambers's *Cyclopedia,* but his preference was for mathematics and astronomy. From 1795 to 1803 he made five long voyages out of Salem. Still he found time to revise an English book on navigation for publication in America in 1799. Then he worked on his own version, which he called *The New American Practical Navigator.* It was printed at Newburyport in 1802. It went through ten editions before his death, and fifty-six more editions since then. Long ago publication was taken over by the United States Hydrographic Survey as its official manual. Bowditch prospered in the insurance business and contributed twenty-three papers on astronomy and navigation to the *Memoirs* of the American Academy of Arts and Sciences. He also translated and edited La Place's *Mécanique Céleste* in four volumes, 1829–39, his notes doubling the length of the original. It was a notable piece of work that made the book available and understandable to American students. But his *Practical Navigator* was his badge and one of the very few early scientific books which has not been superseded by modern research works.

Botany being primarily a descriptive science, it could be studied by self-taught amateurs. Our first native botanist was John Bartram (1699–1777) of Pennsylvania. A farmer, he first interested himself in medicinal plants, then moved on to experiments in hybridization. He opened a correspondence with naturalists in Europe, including the great Linnaeus in Sweden, and exchanged plants with them. As a result Bartram first became well known abroad and later came to the attention of Colden, Franklin, and Washington. He established the first botanical garden on a plot of ground along the Schuylkill River, just outside Philadelphia. It attracted many visitors, who were as pleased by the gentle and knowledgeable proprietor as by the variety of his flora. Bartram managed to travel widely. He discovered the royal palm in Florida and broadened his interests to include shells, insects, birds, fish, and geology. Due to his Quaker religion, he freed his slaves, kept them as paid employees, and had them eat at his table along with his eleven children.

Bartram's principal work was *Observations on the Inhabitants, Climate, Soil, Rivers, Productions, Animals, and Other Matters Worthy of Notice* (London, 1751). Its ninety-six pages resulted from his first trip—up to Lake Ontario to study botany. His botanical garden is now part of Philadelphia's park system.

John Bartram's son, William (1739–1823), followed his father's interest and added an artistic talent. He taught at Philadelphia College, assisted Benjamin Smith Barton and Thomas Say, inspired Alexander Wilson (see below), and influenced such writers as Chateaubriand, Wordsworth, Coleridge, and others. While maintaining the family's botanical garden with his brother, William also managed to travel extensively to botanize and sketch. His work was *Travels Through North and South Carolina, Georgia, East & West Florida, the Cherokee Country, the Extensive Territories of the Muscogulges, or Creek Confederacy, and the Country of the Chactaws* (Philadelphia, 1791). It contained a map and eight plates. The thick book was reprinted in London and Dublin, and translated into German, Dutch, and French. It was also edited for a new edition in 1958. William Bartram was a superb observer of nature and a charming writer. Besides botany, his book contains information on farms, animals, and Indians.

Dr. Benjamin Smith Barton (1766–1815) was a native of

Pennsylvania who obtained his medical degree in 1789 after three years of study in Edinburgh, London, and Göttingen. He then taught at the University of Pennsylvania and turned his attention to flora. His *Collections for an Essay Toward a Materia Medica of the United States* (Philadelphia, 1798; Part 2, 1804) was a pioneering work devoted to medicinal plants. He is also remembered for his *Elements of Botany* (Philadelphia, 1803), the first textbook in the field. It was profusely illustrated from drawings made by his friend, William Bartram.

Perhaps our best-known botanist was Constantine Rafinesque, born in Constantinople to a German mother and a French father in 1783 and privately educated. He was a scientist without scientific discipline; all he had was a lively curiosity and unbounded enthusiasm, along with, unfortunately, an "unconquerable innocence." He came to the United States first in 1802 for two years and did not return until 1815, when he stayed until his death. He went to Lexington, Kentucky, in 1818 and was made professor of botany, natural history, and modern languages at Transylvania University. He was regarded as a brilliant teacher and should have remained in such a position, but he left in 1826 to make his home in Philadelphia, where he died in poverty in 1840. Fish and flowers became his chief interests. He wrote over 900 papers, circulars, reviews, and books. Some are marred by his gullibility, especially evident in his overwhelming desire to discover new species. His major work was a two-volume *Medical Flora; or, A Manual of the Medical Botany of the United States* (Philadelphia, 1828–30). The book contains 100 plates in color of medicinal plants found in the eastern part of the country. In an era when most medical treatment was derived from vegetable drugs, this work was extremely important as a practical reference for physicians and pharmacists.

The acknowledged "father of American geology" was a Scotsman, William Maclure (1763–1840). He came to America on business several times in the 1780s and settled at Philadelphia in 1796, a wealthy man and future citizen. He had already traveled extensively in Europe and Russia to observe geological features. He made a similar tour of New England, Georgia, and Florida, and (it is said) crossed and recrossed the Allegheny Mountains fifty times. His *Observations of the Geology of the United States* was first an article in the *Transactions* of the American Philosophical Society for 1809, accompanied by a colored geological map of the area east of the Mississippi, the first attempt at such a map. The monograph was revised and expanded into a separate book in 1817. His *Essay on the Formation of Rocks* appeared first in 1818 in the *Journal* of the Philadelphia Academy of Natural Sciences, of which he was a founder as well as president for twenty-two years. It too was twice published separately. When the American Geological Society was organized in 1819 at Yale, Maclure was elected its first president. His great legacy was that he stimulated the geological surveys undertaken by the states in their search for mineral deposits. From his work he believed that the Mississippi Valley would be developed entirely as an agricultural region. He also invested money in Robert Owen's utopian community in New Harmony, Indiana, and lived there a couple of years before moving to Mexico.

Another Scotsman, Alexander Wilson, migrated to Philadelphia in 1794, where he taught school and worked as a publisher's editor. More important, he had William Bartram as a neighbor and freedom to read in the naturalist's fine library. Turning his attention to birds, Wilson made notes on those he observed in the eastern United States above Florida. He also sketched them and found an able engraver to work up his drawings; Wilson then colored the plates. His life work was *American Ornithology,* in eight volumes quarto describing 264 species. The first volume appeared from a Philadelphia press in 1808. Seven volumes were published before his death in 1813, and the eighth was ready for printing. Besides his accurate pictures, he wrote engagingly about the habits of the birds. There was no American or European work like it, and ornithologists respect it today. The great French naturalist, Baron Cuvier, declared that Wilson "has treated of

American birds better than those of Europe have yet been treated."

The best-remembered ornithologist of this time, of course, is John James Audubon, who migrated from France to Philadelphia in 1803 when he was eighteen and lived on an estate owned by his father. He had studied drawing and now began observing American birds. Working in trade, he was sent to Louisville in 1807 to manage a store. There he married, neglected business, and began painting birds. He moved to Henderson, Kentucky, took to the woods, and let his partner tend the store. He met Daniel Boone, Alexander Wilson, and Rafinesque. He could not resist sketching some imaginary pictures of strange birds and fish for Rafinesque, who published them as new species. By 1819 Audubon was bankrupt. He floated down the rivers to New Orleans, where his wife supported the family while he sketched. In 1826 they went to Edinburgh, where he was lionized as a scientist. He contracted with Robert Havell, Jr., of London to engrave his bird pictures. They began to appear in parts, elephant folio size (twenty-six by forty inches), in 1827. Eleven years passed before the great work was finished in eight parts, comprising four volumes at $1,000 a set. Meanwhile, Audubon worked up a text to accompany the 435 plates; it filled five smaller volumes and appeared from 1831 to 1839.

Audubon returned to the United States and started a new series, *Viviparous Quadrupeds of North America.* He did about half the pictures before illness overtook him, and his sons completed the work. The two volumes of 150 plates appeared in 1842 and 1845, the text in three volumes, 1846 to 1854. Audubon died in January, 1851.

Only 200 sets of *The Birds of America* were published. The young University of Michigan, moving from Detroit to Ann Arbor and building a campus, managed to buy a set in 1839 which it still has. The attractiveness of the plates as pictures caused many sets to be broken up for individual sales. Waldemar Fries made a survey of the locations of sets, which he published in 1973. He could find only 134 complete sets and 14 incomplete ones. Two copies of the Audubon came on the auction market in 1977. The first brought the unprecedented price of $352,000, which was soon eclipsed by the price of the second: $396,000! Individual plates sell from a few hundred to a few thousand dollars. A set of Audubon is the jewel in any ornithological or natural history collection.

Thomas Say, a great-nephew of William Bartram and son of a Philadelphia physician, was a self-taught naturalist and one of the founders with William Maclure of the Philadelphia Academy of Natural Sciences. When he was thirty-two, Maclure got him appointed zoologist on the expedition of Maj. Stephen Long to Yellowstone. Publication of that expedition's report in 1822 gave Say some recognition, and he was appointed professor of natural history at the University of Pennsylvania. Again Say accompanied Long's expedition to the headwaters of the Mississippi and contributed to the report of 1824. From the two expeditions he was able to compile *American Entomology: or Descriptions of the Insects of North America,* with illustrations in color. Volumes one and two appeared at Philadelphia in 1824 and 1825, and although commended by scientists they were not profitable. The work was entirely descriptive and contained nothing about the life histories of the species he noted and named.

Maclure had become interested in educational reforms possible in New Harmony, Indiana, under Robert Owen. Indeed, he was so far brainwashed by Owen as to believe that "communistic society must prevail, and in the course of a few years Philadelphia must be deserted." Meanwhile, to hasten that day, he agreed to take a faculty of teachers and scientists to the utopian community on the Wabash at his own expense. Say was one of those Maclure drafted to go with him at the end of 1825. After the collapse of the Owenite experiment in two years (whatever happened to Philadelphia?), Say remained at New Harmony as superintendent of the schools Maclure opened. He also married. The third and last volume of his *Entomology* came out in 1828.

Then Say turned his attention to shells, writing *American Conchology; or, Descriptions of Shells of North America.* The six parts were printed on the school press from 1830 to

1834. The illustrations were drawn and colored by Mrs. Say. Say died in 1834, and a seventh part was completed by T. A. Conrad and published.

Farmers in early America were growers rather than agricultural scientists. They learned from experience, but rarely did they write about their experiments. Jared Eliot, already mentioned, was one exception. George Washington was another of our first scientific farmers, experimenting with seeds, fertilizers, and rotation of crops. When he learned that tobacco exhausted the soil, he turned to raising wheat at Mt. Vernon. He corresponded with an American soil scientist, John Beale Bordley (1727–1804), a Maryland lawyer who lived on 1600 acres and experimented widely. Bordley wrote about his work and disseminated his findings on broadsides and printed cards. In 1785, after a second marriage, he moved to Philadelphia, where he organized the Philadelphia Society for Promoting Agriculture. Three substantial volumes appeared from his prolific pen: *A Summary View of the Courses of Crops, in the Husbandry of England and Maryland* (Philadelphia, 1784); *Sketches on Rotations of Crops, and Other Rural Matters* (Philadelphia, 1797); and *Essays and Notes on Husbandry and Rural Affairs* (Philadelphia, 1799).

John Taylor (1753–1824) was a lawyer and veteran of the Revolution who lived on a farm in Caroline County, Virginia. He also served in the United States Senate and wrote several political pamphlets championing states' rights against the national Constitution. On his farm he experimented with crop rotation, plowing under crops, and applying manure to restore fertility of the soil, and investigated the harmful effects of growing tobacco. To a Georgetown newspaper he contributed a series of agricultural papers before the War of 1812. He also wanted to make farmers a powerful political force. Unfortunately, he did not write well. Nevertheless, his essays were reprinted in book form, *The Arator* (Georgetown, 1813). What he had to say was sound enough and made good farming sense.

John Adlum (1759–1836) was a pioneer in viticulture.

After serving in the Revolution, he devoted himself to cultivating European and American grapes, trying to improve a score of native varieties. From cuttings he produced the Catawba grape and lived to see it widely used in wine making. Finally he wrote *A Memoir on the Cultivation of the Vine in America and the Best Mode of Making Wine* (Washington, 1823), the first American work on this subject. An enlarged edition appeared in 1828.

In the area of medicine, collectors thrive on early and modern books that mark progressive steps in knowledge of the human body, diseases, and treatments, medicinal and surgical. It is so large a field that collectors subdivide it by specialties, just as modern doctors do. American contributions were not especially noteworthy in the early days, but they were numerous. Only a small selection can be mentioned here.

Dr. Benjamin Waterhouse (1754–1846) of Massachusetts was educated in London, Edinburgh, and Leyden during the American Revolution. He returned to teach in Harvard's medical department in 1783. Although he wrote on artificial respiration and dysentery, and produced a popular work condemning the use of tobacco and liquor, his claim to fame is that he championed vaccination for smallpox over inoculation. The latter method, introduced from Europe about 1720 over the strong objections of most physicians, gave the patient a mild case of the disease and then immunity. It was difficult to administer and control, and it was dangerous. Vaccination was easier, safer, and did not disable the patient for a time. Waterhouse's argument was set forth in a prophetically titled pamphlet, *A Prospect of Exterminating Small Pox* (Boston, 1800). It persuaded many physicians to use the method.

Home remedy books were best-sellers ever since the seventeenth century. They were a layman's interpretation of medical botany. Perhaps the two most popular works in the colonies were by British physicians: Dr. Nicholas Culpepper and Dr. William Buchan. They were reprinted here frequently. The first one of American authorship was *Every Man His Own*

Doctor (Williamsburg, 1733?) by Dr. John Tennent (1700–1760) of Virginia. The date is in question because no copy of the first edition survives; the second is dated 1734. Knowledgeable in botany, Tennent said his guide was "a plain and easy Means for Persons to cure themselves by medicines grown in America" and went on to recommend it to "those who can't afford to dye by the Hand of a Doctor." (How's that again?) Like some other physicians, Dr. Tennent believed that most diseases had a common cause, and therefore a single cure. He had discovered this sovereign remedy in the rattlesnake root, long used by the Senecas. The House of Burgesses was so impressed by his "discovery" they voted him an award of £100. Four editions of his book were published in Williamsburg, and Benjamin Franklin printed three in Philadelphia. Another appeared in Charleston, South Carolina.

Dr. Tennent discovered that the surest recommendation for a medicine was Indian precedent. The virtue of any American plant was enhanced if it could be said that Indian medicine men used it. This is a distinctively American touch added to home remedies, and it inspired the traveling medicine shows that lasted until well into the twentieth century. One of the first to focus on (and exaggerate) the medical lore of the Indians was Peter Smith (1753–1816), an itinerant Baptist preacher who picked up folk medicine in his travels before he settled near Cincinnati in 1794. There he practiced medicine using roots and herbs. *The Indian Doctor's Dispensatory* (Cincinnati, 1813) by Peter Smith "of the Miami Country" was immensely popular and widely imitated. Patent medicine manufacturers soon found that bottles bearing the word *Indian* on their labels were sure to sell.

It was Samuel Thomson (1769–1843) who established a real cult of botanic medicine followers. Although he had no apprenticeship or formal training in medicine, he used root and herb remedies derived by experimentation. He too believed that "all disease is the effect of one general cause, and may be removed by one general remedy." What was the cause? Cold, or reduction of bodily heat. Therefore, the remedy was botanicals that would induce warmth, plus external "steaming." Thomson patented his "system" and sold it by organizing "Friendly Botanic Societies." Thus, anyone who purchased *The Constitution, Rules and Regulations... of the Friendly Botanic Society... Together with the Preparation of Medicine and System of Practice* (Portsmouth, New Hampshire, 1812) thereby acquired the right to follow the Thomsonian system. The pamphlet was reprinted in Dover three years later. As the number of his societies increased and gathered in national conventions, Thomsonianism became the great vogue. He also inspired two botanical medical colleges.

Inevitably, he wrote a *New Guide to Health* (Boston, 1822) which, published with his autobiography, went through ten editions. There were also separate editions of the *New Guide;* it seemed to be especially popular in Ohio. But before his death the Friendly Botanic Societies grew unfriendly and split into rival factions. Thomsonianism did not long survive its founder, with no loss to the healing profession. Was he a quack? Probably not, because his sincerity was never questioned. He was simply ignorant, while ambitious to help others. In many cases his heat treatment did help; at least it was an improvement on bleeding, which many of the learned profession still practiced.

One of the most popular home remedy books was Dr. John C. Gunn's *Domestic Medicine or Poor Man's Friend, in the House of Affliction, Pain and Sickness* (Knoxville, Tennessee, 1830). Exactly how popular it was is impossible to say with certainty. By the ninth edition, in 1839, the author was claiming sales of more than 100,000. Certainly, this thousand-page book was among the top sellers in the 1850s and after the Civil War, being reprinted in several states. Agents in the Midwest and South peddled it. Several printings in German appeared. In 1885 it carried the notice of its 213th edition!—which is no guarantee of the truth. Its last date is not known.

Dr. Gunn's generous advice included the usual "description of the medicinal roots and herbs of the southern and western country, and how they are to be used in the cure of diseases." He blamed man's declining health on civilization and on the cupidity of physicians in concealing the art of healing "under complicated names, and difficult or unmeaning technical phrases." What distinguished this book, however, was a sizeable section entitled "Of the Passions." Dr. Gunn ventured over the threshold of psychiatry as a counselor in the area of mental health, religion, and love. The passions on which he discoursed were fear, anger, love, jealousy, joy, grief, and intemperance. He pointed out that medicines could not treat the sorrows that spring from the mind; remedies must be found in religion, education, and self-discipline. In the 1850s his book carried colored illustrations of the passions. Surely a book of such comprehensiveness and popularity deserves a place in the history of health practices.

Home remedy books are amusing and astonishing to read, but as their foundation on scientific experience is notoriously weak, the genre need not be pursued further. A genuinely scientific medical work, still respected, was painstakingly prepared by Dr. William Beaumont (1775–1853), an army surgeon, in the 1820s. He was stationed at the fort on Mackinac Island, Michigan, in 1822 when a young French-Canadian fur trader named Alexis St. Martin was accidentally shot in the stomach at close range. Dr. Beaumont saved his life and took him into his own home for convalescence. The hole did not close, but a flap of stomach lining grew over it, fastened only along one edge. It could be opened by pushing with one's finger. The temptation for experimenting could not be resisted, and Dr. Beaumont succumbed in 1825. At that time the process of digestion was not understood, and theories were in wide disagreement. Dr. Beaumont introduced bits of food tied to a thread directly into the stomach and withdrew them from time to time for observation. He proceeded with scientific care and elaborateness and wrote down his findings. His experiments were interrupted for four years by St. Martin's absence and then were resumed. The young man was unaffected by these experiments; he raised a family and at times even exhibited himself by performing such appealing tricks as drinking a glass of milk, then pushing open his valve and letting the milk drain out in full view. He lived to the age of seventy-eight.

Meanwhile Dr. Beaumont wrote up 238 experiments and published them at his own expense under the title *Experiments and Observations on the Gastric Juice and the Physiology of Digestion* (Plattsburgh, 1833). He proved that digestion was a chemical process and that the gastric juice was largely hydrochloric acid and something else, which was soon identified as pepsin. He also showed that gastric juice was secreted only when food was present. He commented on the uses of bile and pancreatic juice. It was a remarkable bit of research scrupulously carried out under primitve conditions. Almost all of Dr. Beaumont's modestly offered "inferences" found their way into textbooks of physiology and are accepted today. His book was reprinted in Boston and Leipzig (1834), in Edinburgh (1838), in Cambridge (1839), and under an altered titled in Burlington, Vermont, in 1847. A facsimile reprint of the first edition was issued in 1929.

Less well known than he should be is Dr. John Sappington (1776–1856) of Maryland and Tennessee, who studied medicine at the University of Pennsylvania under Dr. Benjamin Rush, yet opposed that leading professor's traditional treatment of fevers by purging and bleeding. Dr. Sappington thought it only weakened the patient, as all physicians agree today. When he moved to Missouri in 1819, he found himself in the midst of a malaria region. The next year two French chemists extracted quinine from Peruvian cinchona bark, and in 1822 a quinine factory was opened in Philadelphia. Dr. Sappington used it immediately and enthusiastically with great success. He didn't know a parasite caused malaria or that mosquitoes carried it (neither did anyone else), but he knew that quinine worked in prevention and treatment. Most of his colleagues scoffed.

In 1832 he began manufacturing quinine "anti-fever pills" and in ten years sold over a million boxes of them through drummers who covered the Mississippi Valley. His salesmen, who were required to take three pills a day, never contracted malaria though they moved in regions where it was rampant. Finally Dr. Sappington published his *Theory and Treatment of Fevers* (Arrow Rock, Missouri, 1844) as his legacy to the profession.

Another giant in American medicine was Daniel Drake (1785–1852), who contributed significantly to medical geography. Educated by apprenticeship and at the University of Pennsylvania, where he earned his doctor's degree, he began practice in Cincinnati. Of indefatigable energy and broad interests, he wrote well and lectured effectively. He taught at Transylvania University for a period, took up the cause of medical education, founded the most important medical periodical of his time, and was first to advocate four years of medical training. His crowning work was *A Systematic Treatise, Etiological and Practical, on the Principal Diseases of the Interior Valley of North America, as They Appear in the Caucasian, African, Indian, and Esquimaux Varieties of its Population* (Cincinnati, 1850; 878 pages). It described the character of the population and its illnesses, all done with scientific caution. He was careful in his inferences and wrote in a graceful style. The book was intended to be "a useful manual for daily reference" for his medical colleagues. A monumental work, it was based on Drake's travels, interviews, and reading, as well as his practice.

Historians of dentistry are pretty well agreed that the first dental book published in this country was by Dr. Richard C. Skinner of New York. He had been trained in London and emigrated in 1788. He called himself "surgeon dentist," although he referred to himself as Mr., and the long title indicated the book's broad scope: *A Treatise on the Human Teeth, Concisely Explaining Their Structure and Cause of Disease and Decay: to Which is Added, the Most Beneficial and Effectual Method of Treating all Disorders Incidental to the Teeth and Gums; with Directions for Their Judicious Extraction, and Proper Mode of Preservation: Interspersed with Observations Interesting to, and Worthy the Attention of Every Individual* (New York, 1801). His advice was good, and he warned against unskilled operators specializing in extractions. It is true that Dr. Skinner advertised in the newspaper in 1794 and again in 1796 that he would give to every applicant a free copy of "a small treatise upon the Human Teeth," but no copy is known; probably it was a handbill or brochure.

Historians have noticed the books mentioned here, and others, and have remarked on the tendency of American science to be pragmatic. They see in it remarkable ingenuity rather than profundity. They are inclined to agree with Alexis de Tocqueville, the sharp and reflective French observer who visited the United States in 1831-32. "In America," he wrote, "the purely practical part of science is admirably understood, and careful attention is paid to the theoretical portion which is immediately requisite to application. On this head, the Americans always display a clear, free, original, and inventive power of mind. But hardly any one in the United States devotes himself to the essentially theoretical and abstract portion of human knowledge."

De Tocqueville blamed this deficiency on American democracy. Abstract research requires "meditation," which only a leisure class can provide, he thought. Men who live in a democratic community "seldom indulge in meditation" and "entertain very little esteem for it." They have no time for it because a democratic state and democratic institutions keep men in constant activity, he said. "Equality," he added, "begets in man the desire of judging of everything for himself: it gives him, in all things, a taste for the tangible and the real, a contempt for tradition and for forms." Whether democracy deserves the blame, scientific research has become institutionalized, carried on at universities, in foundation-supported laboratories, or by the federal government, where time for "meditation" is provided.

Most of the scientific titles mentioned above are difficult to find today and vary from moderately to excessively expensive. Yet there are other early contributions in several fields of science that are more readily available. Science lacks the universal appeal of literature, history, or religion. It has a history of its own, but by its nature the latest information is preferred and sought. Since scientists build on the past and discard the disproven, they seldom prize the crude or primitive beginnings of their disciplines. Late in this century the history of science has been recognized as a legitimate and significant aspect of our past by academic history departments. They offer a course or two in it, thereby insuring the survival of early efforts at investigation.

CHAPTER SIX

Music Out of America

THE

New-England Psalm-Singer :

O R,

American Chorister.

C O N T A I N I N G

A Number of Psalm-Tunes, Anthems and Canons.

In Four and Five Parts.

[*Never before Published.*]

Compoſed by WILLIAM BILLINGS,

A Native of Boston, in *New-England.*

Matthew xxi. 16. — *Out of the Mouth of Babes and Sucklings thou haſt perfected Praiſe.*
James v. 13. —— *Is any Merry ? Let him ſing Pſalms.*

O praiſe the Lord with one Conſent, and in this grand Deſign,
Let Britain and the Colonies, unanimouſly join.

Boston : *New-England.* Printed by EDES and GILL.

And to be Sold by them at their Printing-Office in Queen-Street ; by Deacon *Elliot,* under Liberty-Tree ; by *Joſiah Flagg,* in Fiſh-Street ; by *Gillam Baſs,* the Corner of Ann-Street, and by the Author.

Title page (top) and Paul Revere engraving from
The New England Psalm-Singer or Chorister,
composed by William Billings, 1770

CHAPTER SIX

Music Out of America

ARLIER in this century the prevailing opinion in sophisticated musical circles was that America had no musical heritage of its own, no tradition of composition. But when some academic musicologists began investigating early American music in the few libraries that had tried to collect examples, they discovered a store of American composition in the latter decades of the eighteenth century and the early nineteenth, a country music in the main built on the British idiom. According to music historian Irving Lowens, 286 collections were published here before 1810.

What had happened, in brief, was that our native music hardly got started before newer immigrants brought with them a taste for art music from greater European talents that wilted American composition after about 1810. By the twentieth century the first efforts had been forgotten. The true evaluation of American music could only be made by going back to the sources: the tunebooks of the earliest composers.

The American Indian had almost no musical culture. He could and did sing on occasion, but Europeans who heard the racket were not impressed by the melody and certainly not by the harmony, which did not exist. Some of the singing was to arouse fervor for battle, or recite deeds of valor, or lament the dead, or implore divine aid, or thank the Great Spirit for a harvest or victory. The one component the music had was rhythm, for the Indians were devoted to drums and rattles. Thus, there was no aboriginal musical influence on the music brought here by the English settlers early in the seventeenth century. They brought chiefly what they knew by heart: psalms set to popular ballad tunes, romantic Elizabethan songs, and lullabies, all of it country music of the British Isles. Preserving it was the initial problem.

In Massachusetts the English psalter the colonists were using contained seventeen distinct meters, each sung to a different tune. The Puritans felt a need for a simpler psalter for the singing of psalms by the congregation. So a committee planned a literal rearrangement of the Psalms into crude verse of only six patterns of meter which would fit the plain tunes the church members knew best, since there were no organs or choirs to lead them in complex or less familiar melodies. Richard Mather, John Eliot, and Thomas Welde prepared the text, and John Cotton was the prime agent in getting printed at Cambridge 1,700 copies of *The Whole Booke of Psalmes Faithfully Translated into English Metre* in 1640. Collectors prize it because it is the first book printed in the United States (not in America, for Mexico City had a press a century earlier). Only eleven copies are known today, of which all but two are defective, and they are all in libraries. The last one to be sold was auctioned in 1947 in New York. It brought the breathtaking price, for that time, of $151,000 and went to Yale University. The so-called Bay Psalm Book went through about seventy editions before 1774. It was extensively revised in 1651, polishing the versification and adding thirty-six other "Scripture songs." Engraved music was added to the 1698 edition (ninth), or possibly earlier in an edition that has not survived.

Some Puritans had reservations about using the new psalm book. Soon Boston was invaded by Quakers who warned that singing did not belong in a worship service anyway. Two Puritan divines felt obliged to speak up in defense of congre-

gational singing, declaring it to be ordained by God and practiced by the ancient Hebrews. The usual method was for a
precentor or chorister to line out the words and tune just
ahead of the congregation of voices. He had no accompani-
ment.

However, old precentors gave way to new ones, and new
generations grew up who sang the old psalms indifferently or
badly. Melodies were altered or were sung off-key by un-
trained voices and the usual percentage of pious but tone-deaf
worshippers. Not that the congregation thought it was doing
too poorly; it was the clergy up front who got the full blast.
Making a joyful noise unto the Lord was something of an
ordeal for them. Whereas once the people knew many tunes
for psalm singing, they were now having trouble with the
half-dozen called for.

In the eighteenth century three respectable ministers proposed a novel solution: church members should learn again
the tunes as they were written in their psalm books and even
learn to read notes. The full title of the Reverend Thomas
Symmes's anonymously published discourse revealed what
had happened: *The Reasonableness of Regular Singing, or
Singing by Note; in an Essay to Revive the True and Ancient
Mode of Singing Psalm-Tunes, According to the Pattern in
Our New-England Psalmbooks, the Knowledge and Practice
of Which is Greatly Decayed in Most Congregations* (Boston,
1720). Symmes, of Bradford, Massachusetts, suggested singing schools for practice. The Reverend John Tufts of West
Newbury published a little pamphlet called *A Very Plain and
Easy Instruction to the Art of Singing Psalm Tunes* by using
letters to indicate the notes of a scale and punctuation marks
to show their time value. Irving Lowens thinks 1721 was the
date of the first edition, but the earliest known is the third,
dated 1723. The first edition contained twenty-eight tunes;
the fifth grew to thirty-seven. Tufts's pamphlet was much
criticized, but eventually it went through eleven editions.

Cotton Mather called his essay *The Accomplished Singer*,
intended, he said, "for the assistance of all that would sing
psalms with grace in their hearts, but more particularly to

accompany the laudable endeavors of those who are learning to sing by rule." It was published in 1721. Oddly, one man objected by prophesying that singing by rule would be followed by praying by rule, and soon lifeless formality would replace fervency in worship.

To help things along, the Reverend Thomas Walter of Roxbury, grandson of Increase Mather and nephew of Cotton, published *The Grounds and Rules of Musick Explained* (Boston, 1721). Prudently, he had it endorsed by fifteen ministers and printed their names. It was the first book to contain music printed with bar lines. Walter contended that the remembered tunes were now "miserably tortured, and twisted, and quavered, in some churches into an horrid Medley of confused and discordant Noises." Although he died seven years later at the age of thirty-two, his work overcame most objection and reluctance and was reprinted eight times by 1764. It not only contained some psalm tunes, but elementary instructions on how to sing by reading the notes. One effect was that it encouraged the formation of a singing school in Boston for study and practice in 1722, as Symmes had suggested. Here harmony was learned through part singing. Such sessions became social gatherings enjoyable in themselves. Without realizing it, clergymen were responsible for the first instruction books, the first form of musical education, and opened the way for the first American composers.

The small town churches of Massachusetts thought the Boston churches were growing mighty sophisticated to ask their people to learn to read music. Their complaints grew louder when the friends of music suggested having a choir of better voices lead the singing and, of all things, eventually perhaps an organ to accompany them. It was radical enough for an occasional precentor to use a pitch pipe. Organs were used in those Anglican churches which could afford them (New York and Williamsburg first), but to build them in Congregational, Presbyterian, and Baptist churches smacked of Anglican formality and Roman Catholicism. Furthermore, it was easily foreseen that the best singers, who would form the choirs, were those persons who spent their time at singing schools and/or practiced by singing in taverns at night. Were the latter now to be exhibited in places of honor in the congregation?

Good singing ultimately prevailed, and instruction lost its suspect nature. Choirs appeared, and at last people began seriously to study music. Brought over from England, the Reverend Isaac Watts's hymns and psalm tunes became popular here. After about 1750 hymns gradually replaced the psalms for singing. Locally, James Lyon of Pennsylvania saw the trend and put together ninety songs set to a number of well-known English tunes and a half dozen never before published in *Urania, or A Choice Collection of Psalm-Tunes, Anthems and Hymns* (Philadelphia, 1761). A second edition was published in 1767. Lyon was also an advocate of instrumental music in churches.

American composers ventured to lift their heads from surprising occupations. William Billings, a Boston tanner, was only twenty-four when he published his *New England Psalm Singer* in 1770 at Boston. It contained 115 tunes and 5 anthems he had composed. Paul Revere engraved a frontispiece showing several gentlemen gathered around a table with their songbooks, no doubt whooping it up. The book was so well received and Billings so prolific that he published five more songbooks and also conducted singing classes. Indeed, he wrote new, patriotic words to one of his hymn tunes called "Chester," which became a marching song for New England troops during the Revolution.

Lewis Edson, Sr., a Massachusetts blacksmith, was represented in *The Chorister's Companion* (New Haven, 1782) by three fuguing psalm tunes which became the most popular in America of this style of song. His "Greenfield" tune, for instance was reprinted 101 times before 1810. This book and the following ones were still full of sacred music, but were readily used in the growing number of singing schools. Edson went on to become a teacher of singing schools.

More American composers appeared on the scene. Daniel Read, a twenty-eight-year-old combmaker and storekeeper of New Haven, Connecticut, published locally *The American*

Singing Book, which contained forty-seven songs of his own composition intended for use in singing schools. A *Supplement* was issued in 1787. The first title went through six editions before 1797. He published other collections as well, and his tunes were pirated by other compilers. His Christmas hymn, "Sherburne," was reprinted seventy-one times before 1810. Read and Billings have been called the most talented of Yankee composers. Engraver-printer John Norman of Boston put together various psalms and anthems for a *Federal Harmony*, printed in 1788; there were five editions before 1795. Timothy Swan, a hatter of Suffield, Connecticut, is believed to have brought out *The Songster's Museum* (Northampton, 1803) containing 204 pages of secular music, some of it his own. Oliver Holden, a carpenter and bookseller in Charlestown, published *American Harmony* (Boston, 1792) when he was twenty-seven years old. It contained thirteen tunes, all his own. When he issued *The Union Harmony, or Universal Collection of Sacred Music* (Boston, 1793) in two volumes, they contained forty of his own tunes plus the works of many other composers.

Active for more than forty years as teacher, publisher, and traveler, Andrew Law (1749–1821) was the first American to earn his living entirely by music—if you care to call it a living. He was not a composer, but a musician, compiler, and instructor. After graduating from Rhode Island College in 1775 and studying for the ministry, he turned to publishing music, traveling up and down the coast to conduct singing schools and train choirs, directing concerts, and jumping into every musical controversy. It must be admitted that he possessed an abrasive personality—obstinate, suspicious, quarrelsome, and humorless—and perhaps he had no right to expect his profession to reward him more than meagerly. He peddled his song books, accused agents and booksellers of cheating him, complained about printers, assailed his critics, vilified his rivals, fought for copyright, argued forever about shape notes, endured poverty, and remained single, pious, and self-righteous. Law seemed to regard himself as a missionary to elevate American taste and teach everyone to sing.

Indeed, he was so devoted to what he called "the great Masters of Music" (he overlooked the best), that after 1800 he insisted on the superiority of European art music and helped stifle the very American music he had at first accepted.

Law began compiling his first tune book in 1777, a collection of thirty-two songs in four-part harmony entitled *Select Harmony* (Cheshire, Connecticut, 1778), with rules of singing. The tunes were taken from British and American composers. It was followed by a second edition in 1779, enlarged to sixty-five compositions. In it he seemed to champion American composition by including the works of a dozen composers who had never before been published. Revised in 1782, the book saw more than a dozen printings. Meanwhile, he published *A Select Number of Plain Tunes Adapted to Congregational Worship* (Cheshire, 1781), done in four parts. These tunes were of mixed English and American origin. His brother, William Law, a printer in Cheshire, became Andrew's principal publisher.

Law's most important and largest work was *The Art of Singing* (Cheshire, 1794), composed of three separate sections. Because it was issued in four editions over the next sixteen years with double title pages and little regard for consistency in inclusion of parts, the work has been a bibliographical puzzle until Richard Crawford found his way through the jungle of variants in his definitive study of Law. He terms *The Art of Singing* "the most comprehensive vocal method published in America until well into the next century." In the edition of 1803 Law used his "patented" shape notes, omitting the music staff, and for the next decade sought to convince the public of the superiority of this plan.

Shape notes had been devised about 1800 to teach the reading of music at sight, still a problem for instructors. Notes were printed on a staff, but the four syllables—fa, sol, la, mi—were represented by a triangle, a circle, a square, and a diamond. Singers quickly learned to recognize and name them. Law's omission of the staff complicated the recognition and offset the advantage. He went on to prepare for the Methodists *A Choice Collection of Church Music* (Philadelphia, 1807) and he did an instructional work on *The Art of Playing the Organ and Piano Forte* (Philadelphia, 1809), adding three more shape notes to make a full scale of seven. However, his influence and popularity declined after he began printing his books in shape notes.

Law sought to re-form American psalmody in the manner of European musical style, and he succeeded, but at the cost of denigrating the Yankee composers who were ignorant of standards and allowed their creative powers full and natural expression. One effect was the retreat of Yankee music from urban New England centers to the rural South and West.

An inauspicious work of uncertain origin encouraged this retreat. It caught the public fancy in small towns and rural areas and dominated all other music books: *The Easy Instructor, or a New Method of Teaching Sacred Harmony* (Philadelphia, 1801) by William Little and William Smith. Of its 105 compositions, 100 were American, and of them 41 had never before been published and apparently were the work of Smith. But what distinguished the book and accounted for its popularity was the first use of shape notes, two years before Law used them. Unfortunately, shape notes became identified with country people, who welcomed them, and consequently city choir-leaders rejected the system. Further, since those leaders became the first music teachers in the public schools, they kept shape notes out of the classroom and a useful teaching method was ignored. They persisted, however, in song books used in the rural South.

Little, probably a Philadelphia printer interested in music, may have orginated shape notes, but musicologists are not certain. His collaborator, Smith, was obviously a musician, but who he was or where he was located is unknown. After two or three years he defected from the partnership. Little then sold or leased his copyright to some Albany printers who knew how to promote the book. It began to sell widely. A new editor kept revising it every couple of years, deleting American tunes and adding new and fashionable European songs, as well as increasing the pages. *The Easy Instructor* reached its peak of popularity in the second decade of the nineteenth century, even though other compilers turned to using shape notes and plagiarized some of the songs. *The Easy Instructor* continued to be published until 1831.

Down in Pennsylvania an entirely different musical tradition was finding expression among the German settlers. Both Pietists and Moravians (the latter were also in Salem, North Carolina), could recall that Luther, in contrast to Calvin, enjoyed music and wrote hymns; indeed, he saw nothing wrong with instrumental music in church. Consequently, the Germans in America had not only organs, but bands which played for weddings, christenings, and funerals as well as at worship services. They imported European music and practiced singing. Several of their leaders composed sacred music, but unfortunately they rarely published. The result was that this rich and sophisticated music had almost no effect outside the Moravian towns, while Yankee music based on British models was spread up and down the coast by itinerant singing masters and local booksellers.

Lots of popular songs were published and sold here, many of them English and Irish tunes. *Evening Amusement* (Baltimore, 1796) typified the secular music enjoyed by Americans. The book contained fifty airs, duets, songs, and dances "for 1 and 2 German flutes or violins." Most colonial dance music, when not of British origin, was improvised and not written down, even as it is today. A revealing title is *Twenty Four American Country Dances as Danced by the British during Their Winter Quarters at Philadelphia, New York & Charles Town. Collected by Mr. Cantelo, Musician at Bath, where they are now dancing for the first time in Britain* (London, 1785). Brief directions for the couples were included. Obviously some Tory belles had taught British officers new dance steps. This almost unknown book shows the transit of culture back across the Atlantic.

The gap between cultivated and vernacular music, or art and folk music, or city and country music, however one wishes to define it, widened in the early nineteenth century. Americans grew apologetic about their native composers. The composers noted in this chapter are not found in the older dictionaries or cyclopedias of musicians. The vernacular or folk music continued only on the frontier and was rediscovered in the Appalachians in the twentieth century. Meanwhile, another development was affecting American music. The Great Awakening (mentioned in chapter 3) had encouraged the singing of familiar folk hymns. These were religious verses set to secular folk tunes, or melodies everyone knew, largely of English, Irish, and Scotch origin. American composers after 1770 wrote in that style. A Second Awakening after 1800 swept the new West, and folk hymns were preserved there.

Aiming for sales at those revivals and camp meetings, John Wyeth, a printer of Harrisburg, Pennsylvania, put out an anthology including folk hymns in 1813: *Wyeth's Repository of Sacred Music, Part Second.* He used shape notes, too, and offered 149 songs, a few of them English, a third of them new to publication. Many of the latter came from oral tradition and had rough harmonies. The book sold widely along the frontier. It was the first such compilation, although Samuel Holyoke, a singing master of New England, had compiled an earlier border-line folk hymnal in *The Christian Harmonist* (Salem, 1804). He set folk hymn verses favored by Baptists to new genteel tunes of his own composition. Although the book was designed for Baptist churches, it did not reach the frontier and was never broadly used.

Holyoke's volume was barely known to Annias Davisson (1780–1857), a Presbyterian elder and music teacher of Virginia. However, Davisson was familiar with Wyeth's book and drew on it for his *Kentucky Harmony* (Harrisonburg, Virginia, 1815?) of 144 tunes, 15 of which were composed by Davisson himself. The rest of the songs were borrowed from New England composers. He added revival hymns, some of which derived from Negro tunes extemporized at revival gatherings. Davisson offered them all in four-part harmony, with the tenor carrying the melody, and used shape notes. His book was immensely popular throughout the South and went through five editions in ten years. Several tunes from *Kentucky Harmony* are found in church hymnals today.

Surpassing Davisson in popularity was William Walker's *The Southern Harmony,* published for the author in New Haven, Connecticut, in 1835. Ten years later Walker boasted that 600,000 copies had been sold; the seventh edition appeared in 1854. He was the composer of 25 of the 209 tunes, set in shape notes, and the rest were borrowed Yankee tunes and English and Scottish songs. The book was still used in the South in the 1960s.

These three books, by Wyeth, Davisson, and Walker, maintained an American tradition in the Appalachian and trans-Appalachian area, while American musical originality was dying out in the East in the face of European competition. Professional performers were playing and singing European compositions. Taste was elevated. Not until the advent of ragtime and jazz did American composition once again develop a distinctive idiom.

The War of 1812 inspired what has become our national anthem. Attorney Francis Scott Key of Baltimore witnessed the British bombardment of Fort McHenry during the night of September 13, 1814, and wrote a spirited poem about it which he called *The Defence of Fort McHenry.* When it was published as a broadside, he suggested that it could be sung to the tune of an English drinking song, well known in America, entitled "To Anacreon in Heaven." The suggestion was taken up, and the song with the new words became an immediate hit, despite the difficulty most people find in the wide-ranging melody. To help circulation, Benjamin Carr, an enterprising music publisher in Baltimore, quickly printed the words and music together on a folded sheet and gave the piece the title by which we know it: "The Star-Spangled Banner" (Baltimore, 1814). Only ten copies of this first edition are known today, but numerous editions followed. Key was not a musician or even a lyricist, and the music is foreign, yet it cannot be omitted from any account of early American music.

Sheet music publication, of European as well as American composers, got started here in the 1790s, and by 1825 more than 10,000 pieces and editions of pieces had been printed.

Because of the mixed authorship, foreign and domestic, no one has yet determined the dimensions of early American composition in this form. Historians of American culture have a wealth of printed musical material to examine. For generations its extent was not known, but now musicologists are mining it and assuring the social historians of a rich heritage of musical source materials.

CHAPTER SEVEN

The Revolution and Its Issue

COMMON SENSE;

ADDRESSED TO THE

INHABITANTS

O F

A M E R I C A,

On the following interesting

S U B J E C T S.

I Of the Origin and Design of Government in general, with concise Remarks on the English Constitution.

II. Of Monarchy and Hereditary Succession.

III. Thoughts on the present State of American Affairs.

IV. Of the present Ability of America, with some miscellaneous Reflections.

Man knows no Master save creating HEAVEN,
Or those whom choice and common good ordain.

THOMSON.

P H I L A D E L P H I A;
Printed, and Sold, by R. BELL, in Third Street.

M DCC LXX VI.

*Title page of Tom Paine's argument
for independence, 1776*

The Revolution and Its Issue

MONG ACADEMIC HISTORIANS there are several ways of viewing the American Revolution. One may concentrate on the war for independence and try to fathom why Great Britain lost a war it should have won, and conversely why the colonial Americans won a war against such odds. One can regard the war as an anticlimax, occurring after independence had been argued for a dozen years. One can consider it as a disruption of an empire grown too large to be administered with eighteenth-century limitations.

As for causes, one can emphasize political differences or economic restraints. Right from the start, England regarded political control as a logical extension of commercial control, while Americans all along thought that political rights were something different from trade regulations. One can trace the maturing position of the Americans in successive steps as they objected to Parliamentary efforts to tax them and royal efforts to rule them until independence was the inevitable outcome of their stance. One can go on to say that the struggle for home rule ended with the treaty of peace in 1783, and a new struggle over who should rule at home began, climaxing in a Constitution by which conservatives routed the radicals who had prosecuted the war and had produced the democratic Articles of Confederation. I prefer Edmund S. Morgan's perspective that sees the struggle for self-government as a continuing educational process that began in 1764 and was pursued in debate, on the battlefield, and in committee consistently until a Constitution was written in 1787 and adopted. In short, the new government was the fulfillment of the vision of 1776.

The search for self-government within the British Empire was a learning experience for Americans as they plowed new ground. Fertile with new ideas and proposals, they bombarded successive ministries of George III and in turn were answered by tracts or acts embodying old philosophies of empire. This warfare of pamphlets and regulations produced an exchange of more than 225 publications of American authorship before July, 1776, and more than 500 British replies and counterproposals, many of them directed to other Englishmen. To understand the controversy and the successive steps in each side's position, however, it is not necessary to read all this political and economic literature. Historians who have read widely in this corpus of contention have found many repetitions with varying emphases. To comprehend the developing American position, it is requisite to note only a dozen key pieces which reveal the route to independence. It was more a path than a road, cut by these pioneer disputants who were not always sure where they would come out. To some degree independence was a discovery and a surprise, yet in retrospect a logical issue of the controversy.

It is difficult, of course, to measure public opinion in the past. One cannot conduct a poll. One cannot count on editorial opinions, because editorials as they are known today were seldom published in colonial newspapers. A more reliable check is the popularity of certain pamphlets, based on the size and number of editions. If a pamphlet was reprinted several times, it was in response to demand: some people must have been reading it and talking about it and recommending it to friends.

The curtain rises on the drama in 1764. A long and expensive war had ended, called the Seven Years' War in Europe and the French and Indian War in America (where it lasted eight years). Neither label makes clear that Great Britain won Canada and several West Indian islands from France and Florida from Spain, emerging as the most powerful and far-flung empire the world had ever seen. It also had a large war debt, extensive territories to administer and guard, more native populations to pacify, and a new king-emperor. Economically, Britain could tap colonies in a variety of climates for raw materials and find a horde of customers for its manufactured goods in those same colonies. Trade by the colonies outside the empire was forbidden, and smuggling was not to be condoned. This concept, called mercantilism, promised prosperity for the private citizens of both mother country and colonies. The added cost of government and military protection should be borne by taxes on the trade or on the colonists directly—or so thought those in London. Thus a duty was laid on sugar in 1764 simply to raise revenue.

Immediately some Americans raised objections. James Otis, a member of the Massachusetts General Court (or assembly), best expressed these objections in a strong essay, *The Rights of the British Colonies Asserted and Proved* (Boston, 1764). It went through three editions there and was reprinted four times in London. Briefly, he argued that the new duty on sugar was a revenue measure which under English law could not be granted except by the consent of the citizens affected, exercised through their representatives in Parliament. Since Americans had no such representatives, they were being taxed without their consent. Otis was not ready to deny the authority of Parliament over America, but sought to have the Sugar Act suspended.

The British government asked Thomas Whately to reply, and he did so in *The Regulations Lately Made Concerning the Colonies, and the Taxes Imposed Upon Them, Considered* (London, 1765). Whately agreed that taxes could not be levied on British subjects without their consent through Parliament. But it was untrue for the Americans to claim they were not represented in Parliament; they were as much represented as most Englishmen, since three-fourths of the adult males in Britain could not vote because they did not own enough property or lived in towns not eligible to elect representatives. Members of Parliament represented the whole empire, not just the constituency that elected them. Therefore, Americans were "virtually represented."

At the same time, Soame Jenyns, a member of Parliament, wrote *The Objections to the Taxation of our American Colonies by the Legislature of Great Britain, Briefly Considered* (London, 1765). He offered the same arguments as Whately, but he was briefer, delightfully witty, and arrogantly sarcastic. The pamphlet is worth noting only because this is the reply that absolutely infuriated the Americans.

Americans were not impressed by this argument, and when the Stamp Act was passed in 1765, levying duties on all printed or written documents, pamphlets, newspapers, licenses, diplomas, even playing cards, two voices were raised in protest and in reply to Whately and Jenyns. Daniel Dulany, Jr., of Maryland produced *Considerations on the Propriety of Imposing Taxes in the British Colonies, for the Purpose of Raising a Revenue* (Annapolis, 1765). He denounced "virtual representation." It was one thing, Dulany said, to argue that Englishmen who could not vote were represented in Parliament anyway, because they had interests similar to those Englishmen in their midst who could vote; but it did not follow that Americans had interests similar to Englishmen. Indeed, in matters of trade and taxes they were likely to oppose Englishmen, and where was their "virtual representation" then? Dulany's pamphlet was not well written, but it went through five editions in three months. (Dulany himself became a Loyalist during the Revolution and lost his property in Maryland, but remained there.)

The other spokesman was Richard Bland of Virginia, who published *An Inquiry into the Rights of the British Colonies* (Williamsburg, 1766). He offered the first public defense, based on charters and natural rights, of the right of the colonies to tax themselves only through their own assemblies, and the corresponding denial of the right of Parliament to levy on them. This was an advance over Otis's argument. By some historians it is regarded as the most comprehensive and readable of all American protests.

The Stamp Act was also widely viewed as another attack on the security of property, which was regarded as the foundation of liberty. So universal was the concern here that nine colonies sent delegates to a Stamp Act Congress in New York. We know what went on there chiefly because the Maryland delegates allowed their report of the *Proceedings of the Congress at New-York* to be published in Annapolis, 1766. The Congress sent off a petition to Parliament denying its right to tax them. Preparations were made for refusing to buy the stamps and for harassing the agents disbursing them. The result was Parliament's reluctant repeal of the Stamp Act in 1766—not because the petition was convincing, but because the act was not producing any revenue.

Britain had not given up hope of pumping money out of America, and Charles Townshend, the chancellor of the exchequer, said he knew how. Parliament took him at his word, and the Townshend Acts of 1767 laid customs duties on articles that Americans imported: paper, paint, glass, lead, and tea. The duties were to be collected at American ports from merchant importers. This time the colonists organized to refrain from buying such items. It was John Dickinson of Pennsylvania who spoke up now in a series of letters that appeared anonymously in the *Pennsylvania Chronicle* from November 30, 1767, to February 8, 1768, and were reprinted in other newspapers. They were gathered into a booklet: *Letters from a Farmer in Pennsylvania, to the Inhabitants of the British Colonies* (Philadelphia, 1768). It went through seven editions, in addition to the newspaper coverage. Dickinson had little new to say. He reiterated the arguments Dulany had advanced, but with fresh force, declaring that in the Townshend Acts Great Britain was renewing its attack on colonial liberties after retreating from the Stamp Act. He made a distinction between Parliament's right to lay duties in order to regulate trade (which he admitted) and its right to lay such duties in order to raise revenue for general use (which he denied). As late as early 1775, John Adams had not advanced beyond this concept, believing that Parliament could bind America in certain imperial matters affecting the whole empire. Although Dickinson supported the nonimportation agreements, he was opposed to military force and thought reconciliation was possible.

To answer Dickinson, William Knox, a former councillor in Georgia and agent of that colony in England, wrote *The Controversy Between Great Britain and Her Colonies Reviewed; the Several Pleas of the Colonies, in Support of their Right to All the Liberties and Privileges of British Subjects, and Exemption from the Legislative Authority of Parliament, Stated and Considered* (London, 1769). He observed that although the colonials claimed the rights and privileges of Englishmen, they argued that in tax matters they were not the same as the king's subjects in Great Britain. Further, since they acknowledged the supreme authority of Parliament, it seemed to Knox "not worth while to quarrel about the manner of expressing it." Consequently, he thought the distinction between taxes for regulation of trade and taxes for revenue was absurd, as ridiculous as the assumption that the people of England consented to the taxes imposed on themselves. If taxes imposed without consent were illegal, as the American argued, then those who object should not pay. Soon that would be everyone, he pointed out.

What was more apparent was that the Townshend Acts were not fruitful, and at the ministry's behest Parliament repealed all the duties except the one on tea in March, 1770. This was the same month that British soldiers in Boston fired on a taunting mob and killed five civilians. The clash inflamed hostile American feeling against British authority, yet the bloodletting had the effect of quieting extremists on both sides, and a period of false calm followed. The tea tax remained in force, but many Americans refused to buy the product. The uneasy truce lasted until December, 1773, when three British ships entered Boston harbor loaded with tea from India. They were boarded by local fire-eaters thinly disguised as Indians, who threw overboard nearly 350 chests of tea. As punishment, Britain closed Boston's port and outlawed the Massachusetts assembly.

The year 1774 brought onto the American political stage three young men of extraordinary intellect, each of whom set forth his view of the Anglo-American dispute. One was James Wilson, a Pennsylvania attorney, who pointed out in *Considerations on the Nature and the Extent of the Legislative Authority of the British Parliament* (Philadelphia, 1774, but actually drafted four years earlier) that if Parliament had no right to tax Americans then it had no authority over them at all, only over Great Britain. However, both Americans and Britons were subjects of the same king. Basically this was the commonwealth idea a century before England would recognize it.

Thomas Jefferson of Virginia reached the same conclusion in his *A Summary View of the Rights of British America* (Williamsburg, 1774). He emphasized that colonial assemblies were local Parliaments, with sole authority to tax in each colony, and that Americans were subjects of the king by choice. He also introduced the idea that government should promote the people's happiness.

From the Dean of Gloucester, the Reverend Josiah Tucker, came a surprising rebuttal. In *The True Interest of Great Britain Set Forth in Regard to the Colonies* (Norfolk, England, 1774) he listed five possible solutions to the present dispute: (1) suffer things to go on until a favorable opportunity arose for Britain to recover its authority; (2) let the colonies send over delegates to Parliament; (3) declare war on the rebels; (4) let America become the seat of government and send viceroys to Great Britain and Ireland. He acknowledged that there would be objections to all of these. Therefore the best solution was (5) to declare America independent. This would end the political argument and save all the money now spent on administration. Trade, which was the biggest consideration, would not be affected, he declared, because England offered the best market for American raw materials and for the manufactured goods America needed. Tucker was wiser than any politician would admit.

The third American spokesman to emerge was young Alexander Hamilton, a student at King's College (now Columbia) in New York. As active as certain college students in the 1960s, Hamilton harangued campus crowds, wrote inflammatory letters to the local Whig newspapers, and joined a student militia unit for training—yet he protected the pro-British president from mob violence.

The first Continental Congress had met in Philadelphia in September, 1774, and denounced the "intolerable acts" that closed the port of Boston and suspended the assembly; it objected to the stationing of British troops in cities, criticized all the tax measures, listed the rights of the colonists, and urged their continuation of economic sanctions against trade with Britain. Samuel Seabury of New York wrote disparagingly of the Congress in *Free Thoughts on the Proceedings of the Continental Congress* (New York, 1774). He disliked the threatening tone and thought the greatest good would come from submitting to British government and making orderly appeals. As an advocate of national, rather than provincial, action, Hamilton replied with *A Full Vindication of the Measures of Congress* (New York, 1774), in which he asserted that resistance to arbitrary power was both a personal and a community right, deriving from the natural law of self-defense. This right was of divine origin, he said, and existed before governments were instituted.

Up to this time the only independence advocated by American spokesmen was independence from Parliament. But Jefferson had warned that the king, too, could overstep his powers and loosen the last bond of American allegiance. When British troops marched out of Boston for Concord in April, 1775, they met armed resistance and found themselves cooped up in Boston. When they tried to break out in June by attacking the American position on Breed's Hill, they fought a costly battle that did not free them. The second Continental Congress had met in May, "adopted" the New England army around Boston, and appointed George Washington as commander in chief. Still, the active enemy was a "ministerial army," which the king was urged to withdraw.

Dr. Samuel Johnson, literary critic and lexicographer, whose redoubtable pen was for hire, turned out a well-written reply to the hardening American position. It was called *Taxation No Tyranny* (London, 1775). He argued that the Americans had voluntarily relinquished whatever right they might have had to elect representatives to Parliament when they migrated for something they valued more. Further, he asked, if they could create their own Parliaments, why could they not create their own king?

It was a good question. Complete independence was not perceived in the beginning of the conflict, and it was not faced as late as January, 1776. But before the month ran out there came from the press a vigorous argument by one Thomas Paine, a relative newcomer from England and an ardent libertarian, entitled *Common Sense* (Philadelphia, 1776). It pointed out that those Americans who still regarded themselves as loyal subjects of King George fighting a wicked ministry's army were only deceiving themselves. The king agreed with his ministers, said Paine, and was more hostile than they were. There could be no reconciliation short of complete submission. Therefore the only logical course was for the American colonies to recognize the inevitable and declare their independence.

To say that the booklet was widely read is an understatement. Paine had engaged Robert Bell to print 1,000 copies, and the two men would divide the profits from sales at two shillings each. Yet after the first printing quickly sold out, Bell reported no profits. Not surprisingly, Paine found a new printer for an enlarged second edition, but Bell went ahead with a reprint anyway. The title went through twenty-five editions in thirteen American towns before July 4. Bibliographers estimate that there were 120,000 copies in print by then! If one divides 120,000 copies into the 2,500,000 white Americans (including very young children who couldn't read) that is one copy for every twenty-one persons! It is difficult to find another book to compare with it. I once ascertained that if one counts foreign editions and translations of *Gone With the Wind* as if they had all been issued and sold in the United

States, it took eleven years for that novel to achieve the same kind of saturation of one copy for every twenty-one persons in the 1940 census.

The significance of the publication is that by July, 1776, the people of the thirteen colonies were ready to support the action of Congress in declaring them independent. It was a remarkable achievement for one slender book. Where Paine lost reader support was only in his view that even the best government was "but a necessary evil." Americans did not believe that; they agreed with John Adams, whose *Thoughts on Government* (Philadelphia, April, 1776) was a commentary on *Common Sense*. Adams declared (as had Jefferson) that the goal of government is the happiness of society. Although he favored a republic, that form "which communicates ease, comfort, security, or in one word happiness to the greatest number of persons, and in the greatest degree, is the best."

Such were the political ideas of the Americans who led the Revolution in thought. Some historians sum up the long dispute by saying that America had abler leaders than Great Britain had at that time. Independence from Parliament and king was the resolution of the argument, and so the great Declaration was proclaimed to the world, listing "the causes that impel them to separation." Since the colonies had already passed the stage of denying Parliament's authority over them, it was limited to declaring that the king had forfeited their allegiance because of "repeated injuries and usurpations." The indictment listed thirty-one counts against George III. The Declaration was the work of a committee of Congress and largely the writing of Jefferson. Upon its acceptance by Congress on July 4, about eighty copies were printed that night as a broadside by John Dunlap in Philadelphia. Twenty of them survive (several seriously defective) and command an amazing price. Under special circumstances, one sold for $404,000 in 1969; another, in poor physical condition went for $40,000 in 1975. The Declaration was reprinted in broadside form in various towns as a copy arrived. The text also appeared in local newspapers. Washington ordered it read to all his regiments.

As for the war itself, laymen are always surprised at how well documented the military conflict is. The campaigns and battles are recounted by participants, usually by officers and sometimes the highest ranking commanders. Narrative and descriptive journals were published during and after the war.

For instance, the Massachusetts Provincial Congress put together an account of the opening conflict at Lexington and Concord, vividly entitled *Narrative of the Excursion and Ravages of the King's Troops under the Command of General Gage, on the Nineteenth of April, 1775* (Worcester, 1775). It is not unbiased, and it got to London before Gage's report. The propaganda value of the first description of the battles was tremendous, and Gage's corrective was treated with indifference.

After his return home and a Parliamentary inquiry, Sir William Howe wrote an account of his victories at Long Island, White Plains, Brandywine, and Germantown in defense of his alleged lethargy in a *N....rative* that was published in London in 1780. Gen. John Burgoyne tried to explain his surrender at Saratoga in 1777 in *A State of the Expedition from Canada* (London, 1780). Sir Henry Clinton excused his failure at Charleston in 1776 and, skipping over his victory in 1780, went on to explain his failure to move on Newport in *A Narrative of Sir Henry Clinton's Co-operation with Sir Peter Parker, on the Attack of Sullivan's Island in South Carolina in the Year 1776, and with Vice-Admiral Arbuthnot in an Intended Attempt against the French Armament at Rhode Island in 1780* (New York, 1780). The pretended objectivity of the title masked a series of complaints against what he considered to be two stupid naval colleagues. It has recently been republished, with the additions made subsequently by Clinton's hand and edited by William B. Willcox. Clinton was the only commander in chief on either side to attempt a history of the war. His manuscript was not found until the second quarter of this century and was finally printed at New Haven in 1954, edited by Professor Willcox, as *The American Rebellion.* After Yorktown, Clinton and Lord Cornwallis carried on an angry and extensive pamphlet battle, each blaming the other for that debacle.

Lt. Col. Banastre Tarleton, a cavalry commander, published his *History of the Campaigns of 1780 and 1781* (London, 1787). He had been aggressive in the South. Col. John Graves Simcoe, another cavalry leader, published his *Journal* at Exeter, England, in the same year.

Among our French allies, the Comte de Rochambeau, who joined his expeditionary force to Washington's command for the Yorktown campaign, offered his *Relation, ou Journal des Operations du Corps Français* (Philadelphia, 1781). The Marquis de Chastellux related his war experiences in his *Voyages* (Paris, 1786). The Baroness von Redesel, who accompanied her husband on the Burgoyne expedition, wrote her delightful *Letters and Memoirs Relating to the American War of Independence* which appeared first in Berlin in 1800, and in English at New York in 1827. A few other German letters and a journal relating to British campaigns have been published in this century.

In America, Generals William Heath, Israel Putnam, William Moultrie, and Henry Lee wrote memoirs that were published in the nineteenth century. Several *Journals of the Military Expedition of Major General John Sullivan* across New York State in 1779 were gathered and printed at Auburn in 1887. The *Journals of the Continental Congress* were published in thirty-four volumes from 1904 to 1937. Washington's letters were edited by John C. Fitzpatrick in the 1930s and printed in thirty-nine volumes. Kenneth Roberts published ten journals of the expedition against Quebec late in 1775 in *March to Quebec* (New York, 1938). Gen. Nathanael Greene's letters are currently in process of being published. In all, more than fifty veterans have published diaries and memoirs of the Revolution. Two collections of soldiers' letters have appeared in recent years. A new and comprehensive naval history of the Revolution waits on the completion of *Naval Documents of the American Revolution* by the Navy Department.

Maps of the campaigns were published in London during the war to enable the public to follow the distant conflict in a kind of pictorial fashion. The best ones, fifty-four in number, were gathered by Kenneth Nebenzahl in his *Atlas of the American Revolution* (Chicago, 1974), with a historical text by Don Higginbotham. Douglas W. Marshall selected the best *manuscript* maps, made by army engineers for use of commanders, and prepared them for publication in *Campaigns of the American Revolution: An Atlas of Manuscript Maps* (Ann Arbor, Michigan, and Maplewood, New Jersey, 1976).

Though newspapers flourished during the war, they lacked field correspondents and were dependent for battle news on ship captains, passing officers, and rumors. Consequently, their reports are generally inaccurate and unreliable, and must be corrected or corroborated from other sources. They did on occasion, however, print letters of American and enemy officers that are valuable.

All in all, the Revolutionary War was well covered. In spite of these publications and many others, much more source material remains in manuscript form: in the Library of Congress, the Clements Library, eastern historical societies, and other depositories.

Government of the united colonies continued during the war under the Continental Congress, with Articles of Confederation agreed to in 1776, but not formally adopted until March 1, 1781. The Articles defined a central government of delegates selected by the thirteen states, without an executive or judicial branch. The states were suspicious of allowing too much power to a central authority and delayed ratifying even this constitution. The chief stumbling block was not the weakness or strength of the Congress, but the question of western land claims. Some states had old claims in their charters running to the Pacific Ocean; others had none. Since a military victory in which all states fought would guarantee these western claims of the few, the land should belong to all—that is, be assigned to the Continental Congress to pay off the war debt by being sold to settlers, and eventually carved into new and separate states. It was a bold vision. Virginia offered to give up her western claims on this condition, and Maryland, the principal objector to the Articles because she had no western land, was appeased. Ratification came in February, 1781.

The Articles were first printed in eighty copies at Philadelphia in July, 1776, as an eight-page folio. The title read *Articles of Confederation and Perpetual Union, Between the Colonies....* The second issue, in August, changed *Colonies* to *States*. There were nine editions in 1777, and one in 1778. After formal ratification in 1781 there was renewed publication. A first-printing copy is worth a few thousand dollars today.

Attention should be given to one of the last acts of the Continental Congress. It passed a signal ordinance on July 13, 1787, affecting the western lands above the Ohio River, where squatters were already settling and revenue could be derived if some sort of political order was provided. The justly famous Northwest Ordinance was formally *An Ordinance for the Government of the Territory of the United States, North-west of the River Ohio,* printed in New York in 1787. It is only a four-page folder, printed on three sides, and many copies are signed in autograph by Charles Thomson, secretary of the Congress. It was reprinted in other cities. The New York first edition is today worth over a thousand dollars.

What is remarkable about the document is that it neatly solved the problem which had baffled the British government for decades: how to absorb colonies into the mainstream of national government. Britain could never figure out an acceptable mechanism for this transition, without fear of losing face or primacy, until in the 1870s it finally recognized most of its colonies as self-governing dominions under a common sovereign. The Continental Congress could have allowed the West to develop as colonies of the original union of thirteen states, but it was determined to avoid that by creating new states as immigration warranted. So a system was provided for government in three progressive steps: first by an appointed governor, a secretary, and three judges; later, when the population of an area showed 5,000 white males, by an elected assembly under an appointed governor; and finally, when the population reached 60,000, by a state constitution and election of all officials and admission to the Union. The ordinance anticipated that the Northwest Territory would produce three to five new states. The system worked so well that it was applied to land farther west and south, and to Alaska and Hawaii. The Ordinance is original and completely American.

A half dozen years of government under the Articles, in war and peace, revealed the weakness of this loose confederation of the states. Concerned citizens, most of them veterans of the political struggles of the 1760s and 1770s, realized that the newly independent America had not achieved satisfactory self-government. So they called for a convention to revise the Articles of Confederation "to render the constitution of the Federal Government adequate to the exigencies of the Union."

That convention met in Philadelphia in May, 1787, and proceeded not to revise the Articles but to write a new Constitution, more like the state constitutions. The document was finished and signed on September 17. It had been printed in 60 copies on August 6 as a report of the Committee of Detail. It was printed again on September 13 for the Committee of Style. Then 500 copies were struck off on September 17 for the Convention by Philadelphia's John Dunlap, although he had the work done by John M'Lean in New York City. Finally 200 copies were printed September 28 for the expiring Continental Congress to submit to the states for ratification. It had begun appearing in newspapers on September 19. Collectors have a choice of which form to consider the first. Delegate Pierce Butler's copy of the August 6 printing, one of eight copies known, with his manuscript notes, brought $155,000 at auction in 1969.

The Constitution is the true culmination of the American Revolutionary period that began with political argument, proceeded through military warfare, and emerged into trial self-government. It is still a remarkable transition—without a reign of terror (in contrast to the French, Russian, and Chinese revolutions), still worthy of study, still inspiring. It not only legitimized a revolution by the device of approval by conventions, but established a method of transferring power from one majority to another in succeeding generations. Its amendment process obviated the need for any subsequent revolution.

The final great contribution to American political thought is found in the explanations and clarifications of the Constitution offered in a series of eighty-five essays published in the newspapers from October 27, 1787 to August 15, 1788. Although attributions are still disputed, it would appear that five were written by John Jay, thirty by James Madison, and fifty by Alexander Hamilton. They are brilliant essays on the philosophy of representative government and its checks and balances. The United States Supreme Court sometimes adverts to them today. As a result of these explications, the states gradually ratified the Constitution. Before the series ended, seventy-eight of the essays were gathered in book form under the title *The Federalist. A Collection of Essays, Written in Favour of the New Constitution* (New York, 1788; two volumes). Seven more essays, all by Hamilton, appeared in newspapers subsequently. The book has been reprinted many times here and abroad. The first edition is found in thick paper and thin paper states; the former has sold for $5,500, while the latter is worth less than half that sum.

The history of America in the turbulent period from the close of the French and Indian War in 1763 to the inauguration of President Washington in March, 1789, has been written in large part from the source books and documents mentioned in this chapter. They appeared when the ideas and events they embodied were fresh and challenging and exciting. Now that we take so many of them for granted, it is difficult to comprehend how inspiring and sometimes unique were those ideas and victories. The Revolutionary generation felt it had achieved a glorious triumph—and rightly so.

CHAPTER EIGHT

The Westward Movement

T H E
DISCOVERY, SETTLEMENT
And prefent State of
K E N T U C K E :
A N D
An ESSAY towards the TOPOGRAPHY, and NATURAL HISTORY of that important Country:

To which is added,

An A P P E N D I X,

C O N T A I N I N G,

I. The ADVENTURES of Col. *Daniel Boon*, one of the firft Settlers, comprehending every important Occurrence in the political Hiftory of that Province.

II The MINUTES of the *Piankafhaw* council, held at *Poft St. Vincents, April* 15, 1784.

III. An ACCOUNT of the *Indian* Nations inhabiting within the Limits of the Thirteen United States, their Manners and Cuftoms, and Reflections on their Origin.

IV. The STAGES and DISTANCES between *Philadelphia* and the Falls of the *Ohio*; from *Pittfburg* to *Penfacola* and feveral other Places. —The Whole illuftrated by a new and accurate MAP of *Kentucke* and the Country adjoining, drawn from actual Surveys.

By *J O H N F I L S O N.*

Wilmington, Printed by JAMES ADAMS, 1784.

Title page of Filson's Kentucke, 1784, which first publicized Daniel Boone

The Westward Movement

NTIL THE FRENCH and Indian War ended with the surrender of French Canada and eastern Louisiana, the Allegheny and Blue Ridge mountains had been a kind of Chinese Wall to the Anglo-Americans. The coastal colonies facing the Atlantic thinned out to complete wilderness as their western reaches rose higher and higher. The Ohio Valley was known, but it was Indian country. Detroit, Vincennes, and the sparse Illinois settlements were vague oases in a distant land, and New Orleans was almost in another world.

In the 1760s the British army garrisoned those western posts and made the vast region relatively safe for risk-taking fur traders. Two British officers made it known to Englishmen as well as Americans. Capt. Philip Pittman (d. 1775), an acting engineer, was ordered to ascend the Mississippi from New Orleans in 1764. After some delay he reached the Illinois country late in 1765, with a convoy of British troops, and took notes on all the settlements there and made a map of the Mississippi. He visited the new Spanish town of St. Louis. Pittman returned to Florida in 1767 and then to England the following year. For the Colonial Office in London he prepared an extensive report which was published as *The Present State of the European Settlements on the Missis-*

sippi (London, 1770), illustrated with maps and plans. It was the first book on the area by an Englishman who had actually been there.

The other officer, Capt. Thomas Hutchins (1730–1789), was a native of New Jersey who left the army after the outbreak of the Revolution, suffered imprisonment in England, and eventually became "geographer to the United States." It was he who had charge of surveying the Northwest Territory under the land ordinance of 1785. Hutchins had been out to Detroit in 1762, was sent to Illinois in 1766, and became familiar with the whole Ohio Valley. He was ordered to England and produced a geographical work entitled *A Topographical Description of Virginia, Pennsylvania, Maryland, and North Carolina, Comprehending the Rivers Ohio, Kanhawa, Sioto, Cherokee, Wabash, Illinois, Mississippi, &C.* (London, 1778). Its seventy-two pages were illustrated with two maps and a folded table of distances from Fort Pitt to the mouth of the Ohio. How many people bothered to read the book during the war is not known, but Americans had an opportunity to consider the potentials of the region in their deliberations on postwar development.

At the beginning of the Revolution, the trickle of settlers into Kentucky became a torrent. The great popularity of Kentucky was owing to two developments. Virginia claimed it and organized the area into a county, thereby establishing a viable government. Then John Filson (ca. 1747–1788) went there at the close of the Revolution and wrote with enthusiasm *The Discovery, Settlement and Present State of Kentucke* (Wilmington, 1784), accompanied by a splendid map engraved in Philadelphia. The book went through ten editions by 1800 and was persuasive in selling the area to prospective settlers from the East. In an appendix it also publicized the exploits of Daniel Boone, who had been employed by a Carolina speculator, Judge Richard Henderson, in 1774 to open a road through the Cumberland Gap. This narrative increased the popularity of Filson's book. Without this promotion piece, which was not so much a history as a guide, the settlement of Kentucky would have proceeded more slowly. The first edition, with the first state of the map, is worth several thousand dollars today. It was reproduced in facsimile in 1954.

Nothing is known about another author, John Pope. He may have been a Virginian, for his book reveals that he went from Richmond to Pittsburgh, passed down the Ohio and Mississippi to New Orleans, then turned east to Mobile and Pensacola, and up to Augusta and Charleston. His *A Tour Through the Southern and Western Territories of the United States* (Richmond, 1792) describes a section of the country seldom covered in other books. He dealt with Spanish settlements and the Creek Indians as well as the new American West.

Going west meant stepping back a couple of generations in lifestyle. The lack of comforts in housing, the strenuousness of clearing and planting, the danger from Indians, and the scarcity of schools, physicians, and even neighbors were reminiscent of hardships faced by the earliest North American settlers. Yet the promise of starting up rather than starting over toward achievement and wealth made all risks bearable. It is difficult to recapture the excitement of filling that first West: the challenges, the expectations, the movement, the exhilarating freedom, the unlimited hopes. The rich land lay open to the industrious, a new society was stirring to be organized; it was the New World of the sixteenth century all over again, this time faced by pioneers better prepared and under sponsorship more enlightened and helpful. A few contemporaneous books help us today to catch sight of that throbbing world, gone forever.

The great highway into this first West was the Ohio River, surging beyond Fort Pitt all the way to the Mississippi. It was fed by tributaries extending to the north and to the south that encouraged settlement. It had its dangers of sandbars, fallen trees, islands, Indians, and rapids, and Zadok Cramer of Pittsburgh knew it like the lines of his hand. He prepared a modest and practical guide book to the river called *The Navigator,* first printed by him and sold at Pittsburgh in 1801. No copy of the first or second edition survives, an indication of its popularity. The third edition was enlarged under an expanded title: *The Ohio and Mississippi Navigator* (Pittsburgh, 1802), known in but four copies. So popular was it that by 1824 it had gone through twelve editions, even though it inspired several imitators. The book was used like a road map today into a foreign region, but survival, not just direction, was dependent upon it. Besides shoals, channels, rocks, and distances from place to place, it described the Ohio River forts and towns, the Indian tribes that might be met, and the Allegheny and Monongahela rivers which came together at Pittsburgh to form the Ohio. The Mississippi was treated superficially at first, but details were added as the years passed.

If Cramer's guide was deficient in the kind of information prospective settlers of the land wanted, several travelers and explorers supplied a picture of the new country west of the Appalachians. Thaddeus M. Harris (1768–1842), a Harvard graduate and Unitarian minister in Massachusetts, made a western tour in 1805 to restore his failing health. He found the new state of Ohio prosperous, with neat houses, fenced fields, good orchards, and the bustle of trade. Kentucky was less so, even run down. His *The Journals of a Tour into the Territory Northwest of the Allegeny Mountains* (Boston, 1805) was an honest survey of the geography and history of the area he covered.

Fortescue Cuming (1762–1828), an Irishman who had traveled in Europe before coming to America, left Philadelphia early in 1807 and walked to Pittsburgh. He sailed down the Ohio to Maysville, rode horseback through part of Kentucky, and turned northward to Chillicothe, Ohio, then back to Pittsburgh. Starting again, he sailed down the Ohio and Mississippi, crossed Mississippi Territory into West Florida, and ultimately returned to Pennsylvania. He likewise was impressed by the widespread prosperity of the settlers, and noted economic and social conditions generally in his *Sketch of a Tour to the Western Country* (Pittsburgh, 1810).

Jervis Cutler, whose father had helped settle Marietta, Ohio, in 1788, had served as an army officer in the West. He wrote *A Topographical Descripton of the State of Ohio, Indiana Territory, and Louisiana* (Boston, 1812). In it he described the tributaries of the Ohio and Mississippi, the soil, minerals, flora, fauna, and the towns. Briefly he mentioned the Indian tribes on the west side of the Mississippi. One plate in the book is the earliest known view of Cincinnati.

In the same year John Melish (1771–1822) drew on his earlier travels in the Old Northwest to produce *Travels in the United States of America, in the Years 1806 & 1807, and 1809, 1810, and 1811* (Philadelphia, 1812). Born in Scotland, Melish had migrated to Savannah in 1806, then traveled up the coast. Giving up business for travel, he headed west in 1811, went down the Ohio as far as Louisville, and returned to New York via Upper Canada. He was enthusiastic about the area he had seen and wanted to persuade his compatriots to move to this country. His book was reprinted twice here and was published in Ireland and Germany because of its appeal to prospective emigrants.

The prolific Dr. Daniel Drake, a booster of Ohio, focused on his home town and surrounding area in *Natural and Statistical View, or Picture of Cincinnati and the Miami Country* (Cincinnati, 1815), with two maps. Besides offering a brief history of the town, it was filled with meteorological data, descriptions of prehistoric mounds, and notes on medicinal plants and forests.

The extraordinary purchase of the Louisiana Territory in 1803 from the failing tyrant Napoleon doubled the size of the United States. It prompted President Jefferson to find out more about this huge western accretion. He authorized his private secretary, Capt. Meriwether Lewis, and Lieut. William Clark to lead an expedition up the Missouri River and down the Columbia River to the Pacific, and render a report on the geological features, flora, fauna, and Indian tribes encountered along the route. The two officers formed their party or "corps" in Illinois, near the mouth of the Missouri, during the winter of 1803–4. They embarked up the river in May, reached the Pacific in November, 1805, and then largely retraced their route, returning to St. Louis in

September, 1806. Lewis went on to Washington and sought help in organizing his notebooks and specimens.

Meanwhile, from letters received, President Jefferson had sent to Congress his *Message . . . Communicating Discoveries Made in Exploring the Missouri . . . by Captains Lewis and Clark,* dated February 19, 1806. Then Sgt. Patrick Gass, who had kept a diary on the expedition, turned it over to a schoolteacher in western Virginia who rewrote it in an unfortunate "literary" style and got it published at Pittsburgh (by Zadok Cramer) in 1807 as *A Journal of the Voyages and Travels of a Corps of Discovery, under the Command of Capt. Lewis and Capt. Clarke.* The map mentioned on the title page was never issued. In the next five years the book was reprinted five times, including a French translation in Paris. This journal and some of the newspaper accounts of progress were used in a hack-written version of the Lewis and Clark expedition that appeared at Philadelphia in 1809. Lewis was appointed governor of Louisiana, but died in 1809. Clark tried to salvage their unfinished report, but was not equal to it and secured the editorial help of banker Nicholas Biddle and journalist Paul Allen of Philadelphia. They took their time (too much) and finally the official *History of the Expedition Under the Command of Captains Lewis and Clark* appeared in two volumes at Philadelphia in 1814. Over 1400 copies were printed. This work remains the prized report, even though Reuben Gold Thwaites edited and published all the extant journals of the expedition in eight volumes in 1904-5. At the auction of Thomas Streeter's books in 1967 a particularly fine copy of the 1814 set in original printed boards, uncut, brought the unprecedented sum of $35,000. Since then other copies, rebound, have sold for a quarter to a third of that figure.

Before the Biddle-Allen edition appeared, Lieut. Zebulon Pike, also sent out by President Jefferson, had overlapped part of the Lewis and Clark route on a long trip, 1805-7, to find the source of the Mississippi and then westward to the Rockies and back south. He spotted a towering peak in

Colorado that was named for him. Pike was captured by Mexicans, but after his release he prepared his own report that was published as *An Account of Expeditions to the Sources of the Mississippi, and Through the Western Parts of Louisiana to the Sources of the Arkansas, Kansas, La Platte, and Pierre Jaun Rivers* (Philadelphia, 1810). It was primarily a scientific survey in the manner of Lewis and Clark. Reprinted in London, it was also translated into French, Dutch, and German before 1814.

With these works a second West, beyond the Mississippi, came into public consciousness. After the War of 1812, which left the several Indian tribes who had allied themselves with the British defeated, migration to the Mississippi filled the first West and created several new states in short order. Concentration of national attention on westward expansion meant that America turned its back on Europe. The Great Plains beckoned, and the Rockies were a challenge. The second West was not left alone between Lewis and Clark and the Gold Rush of 1849—far from it. It was entered early, but only a few of the venturesome can be mentioned here.

James O. (for Ohio) Pattie of Missouri accompanied his father across the plains in 1823 to Santa Fe. They engaged in the fur trade, and for the next six years James roamed through the Spanish Southwest, including New Mexico and California. In the latter province they were imprisoned, and the elder Pattie died in San Diego. When James returned east in 1830, he recounted his wanderings in great detail to Timothy Flint, a Cincinnati publisher. The resulting collaboration produced *The Personal Narrative of James O. Pattie, of Kentucky, During an Expedition from St. Louis Through the Vast Regions Between that Place and the Pacific Ocean*, edited by Flint (Cincinnati, 1831). It was not a book to appeal to emigrants. Pattie's recall was so good that the book's validity has been questioned. Some details are inaccurate, but they may be Flint's fault rather than Pattie's fiction. The 1833 edition is the same book with a new title page which Flint's nephew added to the unsold sheets of the 1831 edition. None of them could have anticipated that the second edition would sell for a thousand dollars in 1979, while the first would bring ten times that amount.

Zenas Leonard was a mountain man. He had been born in the Alleghenies of Pennsylvania in 1809 and left home deliberately to pursue the Rocky Mountain fur trade. From 1831 to 1836 he roamed beyond the fringe of settlement, trading and hunting, meeting Indians and traders at rendezvous for trade. He was also in Captain Bonneville's party, the first to cross the Sierra Nevada Mountains into California and see the giant redwoods. The *Narrative of the Adventures of Zenas Leonard* was published at Clearfield, Pennsylvania, in 1839. It is a fundamental source for exploration of the Far West and for this style of fur trading. Extremely rare, the first edition has sold for $12,000. Leonard established himself as a trader in Missouri and died there in 1857.

In the early 1830s, long before the discovery of gold in Spanish California, an Oregon fever infected many Easterners, induced largely by a dispute between Great Britian and the United States over ownership of the region. The rich soil, the great timber, and the mild valleys aroused the enthusiasm of the restless. The famous Oregon Trail began in Kansas after leaving Independence, Missouri. It wound northward into the future Nebraska beside the Platte and North Platte rivers to Fort Laramie, Wyoming. West of that post it crossed the first range of the Rockies via the South Pass; then the California Trail branched off southwest to the future Carson City, Nevada, and across the Sierras to Sacramento. The Oregon Trail led northwest up across southern Idaho beside the Snake River to Fort Boise. Crossing the Blue Mountains it reached Fort Walla Walla and followed the Columbia River past the Willamette Valley, where most of the early pioneers settled. The first emigrant train of wagons went over the long trail in 1842. For the next several years the number of trains increased every year, until the discovery of gold in California in 1848 deflected movers to the California Trail.

The general American public first learned about Oregon from *Travels in the Great Western Prairies, the Anahuac and*

Rocky Mountains, and in the Oregon Territory in 1841. The book was written by Thomas J. Farnham, who left Peoria, Illinois, with a local party on May 1, 1839. They took the Santa Fe Trail to Bent's Fort on the upper Arkansas River (near Rocky Ford, Colorado), where Farnham and four others turned and rode north to the North Platte River. With a Snake Indian guide, Farnham went up the Green River (in eastern Utah) and reached Fort Hall (north of Pocatello, Idaho) on September 1. He came to Whitman's Mission post (near Walla Walla, Washington) and explored Oregon, even going up to Vancouver. His roundabout route was not the later, popular Oregon Trail. In December he left Oregon for Hawaii, but was in New Orleans the next summer, having crossed southern Mexico to the Gulf. He ascended the Mississippi back to Illinois, where he composed his book; the preface was signed at Tremont, Illinois, on October 1, 1840. It was published at Poughkeepsie, New York. His comments on Oregon were far from enthusiastic. He found only a little of the land arable, the climate "unfavorable to great productiveness," and the mineral resources still unknown. The book was reprinted in 1843 at New York. Farnham returned to California subsequently and died there in 1848, at the age of forty-four.

Adding to the adventurous appeal of the West were two impressive picture books of the Plains Indians. Prince Maximilian of Wied-Neuwied, a wealthy naturalist, went up the Missouri River in the summer of 1833. He reached Fort Union, Montana, (close to the North Dakota line, at the mouth of the Yellowstone River) and took a keelboat on to Fort Mackenzie (Loma, Montana, at the mouth of the Marias River). He spent the winter back at Fort Clark, North Dakota, fifty miles north of Bismarck, among the Mandan Sioux, returning to St. Louis in May, 1834. In his entourage was a Swiss artist, Karl Bodmer, from whose paintings eighty-one plates were engraved and colored for an atlas published with the prince's book: *Reise in das Innere Nord-America* (Coblenz, 1839). It was reprinted in Paris and London in 1843. Important and beautiful as this work is today, how well known it was in the United States is questionable; and it was overshadowed by the second book, by George Catlin.

Catlin (1796–1892) was trained in law, but turned to painting, particularly portrait work. After 1830 he devoted himself to preserving the likenesses and way of life of what he believed to be a vanishing race. At least its primitive culture was doomed, and each summer Catlin went west to paint until by 1839 he had 600 portraits of Indians and pictures of villages, tepees, games, religious ceremonies, and other aspects of native life. He exhibited his pictures in the East and abroad. Although he was not as good an artist as Bodmer, his *Letters and Notes on the Manners, Customs, and Condition of the North American Indians* was published in London, 1841, with 309 plates in two volumes. It was reissued the same year in New York from the English sheets. Catlin sold his plates to H. G. Bohn, who published them in London with Catlin's text under a different title in 1848. The tenth edition appeared in 1866, and another in 1876. In 1845 Catlin had had published some more pictures in a *Portfolio*. He lost his money in 1852 in a speculation and borrowed privately, pledging his collection of pictures as collateral. Catlin was never able to repay the loan and redeem them; they were eventually given to the Smithsonian Institution. However, he had painted copies of 220 of them, which are now in the New-York Historical Society.

John C. Frémont was an unknown army lieutenant in the engineering corps, married to the daughter of the powerful Sen. Thomas Hart Benton of Missouri, an ardent expansionist. During the summer of 1842 he was sent on a mapping and scientific expedition up the North Platte River, through South Pass, and to the headwaters of the Green River. His report, polished by his talented wife, was published by the United States Senate in 1843 as *A Report on Exploration of the Country Lying Between the Missouri River and the Rocky Mountains*. Running more than 200 pages and containing a map, it was extremely popular and went through several reprints.

His second exploration, in 1843 and 1844, took him to

Colorado, the Great Salt Lake, Oregon, and Mexican California. Now a captain, Frémont added four small maps and one large folding map to his report. It was ordered published in 10,000 copies by Congress in 1845, along with a reprint of his first book: *Report of the Exploring Expedition to the Rocky Mountains in 1842, and to Oregon and California in the Years 1843–44.* In addition to his wife's editorial help, Frèmont had enjoyed invaluable assistance from two wilderness experts, Kit Carson and Tom Fitzpatrick. His reports popularized the West and gave it a romantic glow. The work was drawn on later by publishers of guidebooks issued during and after the Gold Rush. Frémont led California's revolt against Mexican rule, and he had high political ambitions that were never realized.

Meanwhile, Lansford W. Hastings of Mt. Vernon, Ohio, had led a large emigrant train to Oregon in 1842. The movers left Missouri on May 15 and arrived in the Willamette Valley on October 5. Hastings went on to California the next May, ambitious to make a fortune or lead a revolt against Mexican rule. He lacked the talent to do either, but he could see all kinds of opportunities for smart operators, and so he wrote a booster book about the Far West. Returning to Ohio with it in 1844, he got it published the next year in Cincinnati as *The Emigrants' Guide, to Oregon and California,* in paper wrappers. Less than a dozen copies seem to have survived. What distinguished the book was his detailed description of different routes and his listing of equipment and supplies needed for the trek. He was optimistic and even misleading about prospects, but his directions were exact and easy to follow. Five editions were published in the next dozen years. If Frémont helped create a mythical West of enormous enchantment, Hastings told how to get there and what to take along.

A Whig editor from Columbus, Ohio, succumbed to Western fever in 1841. Rufus B. Sage accompanied a fur trading party headed for the Rockies and returned to Missouri the following summer. Promptly he took off again down the Santa Fe Trail, then like Farnham turned north to the Platte River of Nebraska, where he spent the winter. He ran into

Frémont in 1843. The next year he returned to the Arkansas River and then back east. His *Scenes in the Rocky Mountains, Oregon, California, New Mexico, Texas, and Grand Prairies* was published at Philadelphia and New York in 1846. If perhaps he had not visited all those places, he had learned a good deal about them in three years of travel, and, of course, he could write well. Some copies, but not all, contain a map which showed the earliest delineation of "Ne-bras-ka," making it a very rare and desirable map of the western country. A second edition of the book appeared the next year, and a third in 1857.

A fresh note in western travel was injected by two former Wabash College boys. Overton Johnson did not finish his junior year in 1841 before going to Missouri to visit William Winter, who had been in college the year before. The two of them made plans for a western adventure which matured two years later. They left Independence, Missouri, in May, 1843, and arrived at Oregon City in November. Winter went down to California, but seems to have returned temporarily before Johnson started back east in April, 1845. He had Winter's notes with him, and back in Indiana he wrote up the joint work under the title of *Route Across the Rocky Mountains, With a Description of Oregon and California*. It was published at Lafayette, Indiana, early in 1846. Like the Hastings book, the last pages contained instructions, an itinerary, and needed supplies. More important was their statement, "Gold is found in considerable quantities" in California. Johnson died in Indiana in 1849, but Winter prospered in the West and died in Idaho in 1879.

Another Hoosier, Joel Palmer (1810–1881), constructed part of the Whitewater Canal in southeastern Indiana and served a term in the Indiana General Assembly. Then he went to Oregon in 1845, keeping a diary along the way. He returned to Indiana late in 1846 and wrote his *Journal of Travels Over the Rocky Mountains, to the Mouth of the Columbia River*. It was published at Cincinnati in 1847 in the middle of the war with Mexico and ran to 189 pages. Historian Reuben Gold Thwaites called it the best account of the Oregon Trail, adding that it was detailed enough to be used as a guide. Three more editions appeared in the next five years. Palmer took his family and guided a train of ninety-nine wagons to Oregon again in 1847, founded the town of Dayton, became superintendent of Indian affairs, then was elected to the Oregon legislature and remained prominent the rest of his life.

Adventure stories supplanted guide books as the trails west became well known and marked. Representative of them was *Life on the Plains and Among the Diggings,* published at Auburn and Buffalo in 1854, by Alonzo Delano. He had moved from Auburn to South Bend, Indiana, where he heard of the gold strike. He set out for California in April, 1849, and was a sharp observer as well as a good writer. He supported himself not by finding gold but by writing pieces for eastern newspapers. After he returned east in 1852, he wrote his popular account, full of anecdotes. Soon after it was published he went back to California, where he became a prosperous banker and humorous author until his death in 1874. His book was reprinted at New York in 1857 (called the "fourth thousand"), 1859, and 1861. In this century it reappeared in 1936.

The foregoing titles are samples of a distinctive literary tradition that reflects the crossing of a continent. Writings on the Far West continued to pour out. The famous bibliography, *The Plains and the Rockies,* by Henry R. Wagner and Charles L. Camp, in its third edition in 1953, listed 537 titles printed between 1800 and 1865. Even after one subtracts 56 of them as articles in periodicals, 78 as government reports, and a few broadsides, there remain nearly 400 books on the area. They gave an epic quality to the westward movement. They inspired western fiction from then on and classic western films. Expansion was well documented, with all its hardships, disasters, enemy attacks, heroics, failures, and triumphs.

Moreover, these works were almost all by amateurs. The guidebooks and surveys were purposely pragmatic, but the others were records of personal experiences. For the most part the books were the only ones the authors ever wrote.

They reveal certain traits: courage, self-reliance, resourceful-ness, and adaptability, which we like to think of as American characteristics. They comprise a folk literature attractive to every new generation. They are perennially rediscovered.

Without knowing it, these adventurous movers were shaping the future of their young country, for good and evil. From their accounts the historian learns more than routes and hardships. He comes to grips with "manifest destiny" outside its rhetorical ring in the halls of Congress. Was it a noble vision, or a grab for more land, ignoble, covetous, and self-centered? What was supposed to happen to the Indians, and what did? Did Mexico deserve to keep its misgoverned northern districts? How did all this vacant land affect recon-struction in the South, the growth of railroads, immigration from Europe and Asia, and foreign trade? Some universities, recognizing the importance of this continental expansion, offer a separate course in the history of the westward move-ment. It has enchanted literary as well as social historians.

CHAPTER NINE

Sports in America

Illustration from Frost's manual
The Art of Swimming, *1818*

Sports in America

MERICA had an attraction to British commoners that is never mentioned in textbooks. Much has been written about the quest for religious freedom and the appeal of ample land, and these were powerful magnets for those interested in economic and spiritual improvement. Ownership of extensive land marked the aristocracy of Great Britain, and the ordinary folk could not aspire to it there; not enough land was available. Along with their land, the nobility also enjoyed the distinction of being able to hunt and fish at will. These sports were the privilege of gentlemen; they were the very evidence of status.

The settler in America quickly discovered that regardless of how much land he owned he was as free to hunt and fish as any nobleman back home. A few of the promotional tracts advertising America made this point. Only in the wilderness of the New World could a man's social status rise so steeply.

The Puritan objection to the theater did not extend to all other amusements or sports. William Pryne, who in 1633 published in London the prime attack on the theater, suggested such alternative recreations as "walking, riding, fishing, fowling, hunting, ringing, leaping, vaulting, wrestling, running, shooting, singing of psalms and pious ditties, playing upon musical instruments, sating of the bar, tossing the pike, riding of the great horse (an exercise fit for men of quality), running at the ring, with a world of such like laudable, cheap, and harmless exercises."

Fishermen like to fish together, so it is not surprising to find in Pennsylvania the Schuylkill Fishing Company, formed in 1732 by twenty-seven gentlemen of Philadelphia. Its activities were social as well as sporting, having quarters after 1748 in a building called the Court House, close to the river. Fish dinners were held there, preceded by the club's famous Fish House Punch. The group's history was prepared and published by William Milnor, Jr., on what was close to its centennial. His work is *An Authentic Historical Memoir of the Schuylkill Fishing Company of the State in Schuylkill* (Philadelphia, 1830).

The first publication on fishing was not a manual or a guide, but a sermon giving clerical approval to angling. It was printed at Boston in 1743 under the pseudonym of Fluviatulis Piscator. He was the Reverend Joseph Seccombe. His title was a little evasive: *Business and Diversion Inoffensive to God, and Necessary for the Comfort and Support of Human Society.* What is he talking about? The subtitle gives a hint: *A Discourse Utter'd in Part at Ammauskeg-Falls in the Fishing Season.* The date of 1739 is given; it had taken four years for Kneeland and Green, the printers, either to gather enough courage to publish such a sermon or to obtain the pastor's approval.

One of the most popular fishing guides was written by John J. Brown, but published anonymously. It was *The American Angler's Guide. Being a Compilation from the Works of Popular English Authors from Walton to the Present Time. Together with the Opinions and Practices of the Best American Anglers* (New York, 1845). There are chapters on rods, hooks, lines, baits, sinkers, and artificial flies, followed by chapters on various fish, their locations and habits, and how best to catch them, which the author calls the "art of angling." Would any fisherman disagree? The book concludes with the usual fish stories and anecdotes of success. It went through six editions in the next dozen years. The reason for anonymity appears at the end, where there are five pages of advertisements for fishing tackle of all kinds, from John J. Brown and Co.!

The author of the first book on hunting is unknown. He did not treat hunting as a livelihood or as a means of feeding a family, but strictly as a sport. The title was *The Sportsman's Companion; or, an Essay on Shooting; Illustriously Showing in What Manner to Fire at Birds of Game, in Various Directions and Situations—and, Directions to Gentlemen for the Treatment and Breaking Their Own Pointers and Spaniels, by a Gentleman* (New York, 1783). There were two more editions, published at Burlington, New Jersey, in 1791, and Philadelphia, in 1792.

A generation later appeared *The American Shooter's Manual, Comprising Such Plain and Simple Rules as are Necessary to Introduce the Inexperienced into a Full Knowledge of All that Relates to the Dog, and the Correct Use of the Gun* (Philadelphia, 1827), a small book, duodecimo, of 250 pages and three engraved plates. Although published anonymously— "By a Gentleman of Philadelphia County"—it has been attributed to Dr. Jesse Y. Kester. The book was reprinted the following year.

Fishing and hunting, to be sure, are noncompetitive sports, unlike athletic games, races, and other contests. The first book on a competitive sport printed in this country was a text on fencing. It appeared at Williamsburg in 1734. Written by Edward Blackwell, the book's title reads *A Compleate System on Fencing: or, the Art of Defence, in the Use of the Small-Sword, Wherein the Most Necessary Parts Thereof are Plainly Laid Down; Chiefly for Gentlemen, Promoters and Lovers of that Science in North America.* The work is a thorough reworking of an English text printed in London in 1702 and 1705, with a preface and dedication addressed to Americans. The English text was by Henry Blackwell, whose relationship to Edward Blackwell is not known; but Edward was in America and had died recently, for his book was printed for the benefit of his widow and children. The next

American manual on fencing seems not to have appeared until 1823.

These titles should not be regarded as the first *references* to sport in America. Ralph Hamor, who migrated to Jamestown, in 1610, returned to London in 1614 to write *A True Discourse* of Virginia. In the booklet he reported that Gov. Sir Thomas Dale, on his arrival in Jamestown in 1611, found too many inhabitants idle and put an end to "their daily and usual works, bowling in the streets." A few years later the Dutch settlers in New Amsterdam were rolling balls on a spot still called Bowling Green.

Although the American Indians were inveterate gamblers, they seem to have had only one team sport. The number of players on either side was unlimited. The game was played with a wooden ball, and each player used a hickory stick having one end bent around in a curve and strung with a net of rawhide strings for catching and throwing the ball. The object was to pass the ball and throw it over the opposing team and beyond some sort of goal line. It was a rough game, players were injured, heavy wagers were made, and sometimes a whole village played against another village. The game is mentioned in the Jesuit *Relation* of 1636, and Charlevoix saw it played in the middle of the eighteenth century. French witnesses were reminded of a somewhat similar game played in France with sticks curved like a bishop's crozier; it was called *le jeu de la crosse*. Not surprisingly, the French Canadians dubbed the Indian game lacrosse and eventually gave it some humane rules.

Once, in 1763, the game was used by the Chippewas, who called it *baggataway,* as a ruse for gaining entrance to Fort Michilimackinac (Mackinaw City, Michigan) by throwing the ball over the stockade and rushing with whoops pellmell through the gate to retrieve it. Once inside they took guns from their blanketed squaws, killed over half the garrison, and captured the fort. It was their contribution to Chief Pontiac's uprising at Detroit against the British. One of the victims who survived, Alexander Henry, told the story in detail in his *Travels and Adventures in Canada* (New York, 1809).

Montreal formed a lacrosse club in 1839 and played Indian teams. Dr. William George Beers of Montreal published rules for *The Game of Lacrosse* (Montreal, 1860) in a pamphlet, perhaps the first time they appeared in print.

Possibly the second book devoted to a sporting subject printed in this country, and illustrated with American woodcuts, was Philip Astley's *The Modern Riding-Master: or, a Key to the Knowledge of the Horse and Horsemanship . . . Adorned with Various Engravings* (Philadelphia, 1776), taken from the London (1775) edition. It was printed and sold by Robert Aitken, the King James Bible publisher mentioned in chapter 3. An Englishman and ex-cavalry officer, Astley was a superb rider and teacher who pioneered in riding exhibitions, which, with clowns and acrobats added, inaugurated the English circus. He was undoubtedly the best horse tamer of his time. He said he cared little about the breed or shape or color of a horse, only its temper—this from a man noted for his own violent temper and rude manners. Incidentally, Astley's English circus was introduced to this country by men he had trained.

Golf was played in the fifteenth century in Scotland, where the Royal and Ancient Golf Club of St. Andrews, founded in 1774, eventually set the rules accepted throughout the world. The South Carolina Golf Club was organized in Charleston in 1786, but died out about 1810. Savannah had a golf club in 1795 that expired about 1820. It is thought that the game was learned by young Carolinians sent to English universities. The two clubs are known only from newspaper advertisements of social and business meetings. The game was revived in 1887 when a links was opened near Yonkers, New York.

Other sports attracted writers and teachers. Thus J. Frost issued *The Art of Swimming; a Series of Practical Instructions* (New York, 1818). It was illustrated with twelve engravings to show various strokes. Swimming was recommended as a recreation and for health. A dozen years later was published *The Archer's Manual: or, the Art of Shooting with the Long Bow, as Practised by the United Bowmen of Philadelphia* (Philadelphia, 1830). Meanwhile, the first sports periodical had been started in 1829: *American Turf Register and Sporting Magazine*. It was a monthly that began in Baltimore and continued in New York for fifteen years, under four different editors. It was proof that horse racing attracted crowds which would support such a magazine.

Pugilism is an ancient sport that died out after the fall of Rome. It was revived in England in the eighteenth century with strict rules and padded gloves. In America the first boxers were slaves. The first professional fight among whites seems to have been between Jacob Hyer and Tom Beasley in 1816. Hyer won and claimed the championship. He boasted he could "lick everybody else in America," but promptly retired and never fought again. His son Tom took up the "manly art" and achieved what he called the championship in 1849 by knocking out "Yankee" Sullivan (actually an Irish boxer on tour) in the sixteenth round. Then, like his father, he quickly retired. Someone, under the pseudonym of Patrick Timony, immortalized him by writing a pamphlet, *The American Fistiana: Containing a History of Prize Fighting in the United States . . . and a Full and Precise Account . . . of the Great $10,000 Match between Sullivan and Hyer* (New York, 1849). These were bare-knuckled fights, which practice persisted here until about 1890.

Cricket has been played in England since the Middle Ages. It was regularized in London in 1787 by the founding of the Marylebone Cricket Club, which still governs the sport. It was played in America first in 1747, but did not attract attention. British officers played cricket, it is said, during their occupation of Philadelphia in 1778. A revival of interest occurred in the 1830s, and the Philadelphia Union Cricket Club was formed in 1832, but dissolved in 1846. Up in Massachusetts the Worcester Cricket Club published *The Laws of Cricket as Revised by the Marylebone Cricket Club and Adopted by the Worcester Cricket Club* (Worcester, 1857). The game was soon overwhelmed by baseball.

Some of our games of sport are of too recent development in the United States to be considered here. Football was a post-Civil War variation of an earlier English school game. Tennis was introduced from England in 1874. Ice hockey came to us from Canada in the 1880s. Basketball is an American invention of 1891 at a Springfield, Massachusetts, YMCA school.

Now for baseball. The game was not originally an American invention, and it was not created by Abner Doubleday at Cooperstown, New York, in 1839. It is undoubtedly much older. The New York printer, Hugh Gaine, reprinted in 1762 a small English book of 1744 entitled *A Little Pretty Book. Intended for the Instruction and Amusement of Little Master Tommy and Pretty Miss Polly.* It was the first juvenile published in London by John Newberry, whose name graces the Newberry Medal today for the best children's book published each year. This eighteenth-century Dick and Jane book was illustrated with small woodcuts. No copy of Gaine's books has been found, but it is known from a newspaper advertisement. The London (1744) edition shows fishing, but another cut shows baseball—unmistakably. Boys are playing a game with ball, bat, and bases or posts to run to after hitting the ball. The picture is even captioned "Base-Ball." Isaiah Thomas reprinted the London edition at Worcester in 1787 with its sixty-five illustrations.

Baseball was played by the soldiers at Valley Forge in 1778. Princeton, or the College of New Jersey, had teams in 1786. It may not have been quite the same game, as there was no uniformity of rules. Jane Austen spoke of baseball in her 1798 novel. It remained for an Englishman, William Clarke, to publish the first set of rules in 1829 for a game called "rounders," which actually was baseball. Those rules were reprinted in Boston as part of Clarke's *Boy's Own Book* (first American edition, 1829).

Rochester, New York, had a baseball club in 1825, and the game was played at Brown University in 1827. Robin Carver described baseball in *The Book of Sports* (Boston, 1834). The Knickerbocker Base Ball Club was organized in New York

City in 1842 and issued new rules three years later, along with a diagram of a diamond. The sport was now further organized with the formation of other clubs and issuance of invitations for intercity games. The object of the game was to complete twenty-one runs, rather than nine innings.

The first genuine sportswriter in America, who devoted himself to writing about sporting activities in general, was "Frank Forester," the pseudonym of Henry William Herbert (1807–1858), an Englishman who migrated to this country in 1831. His first vocation was teaching (he was a classical scholar); then he began writing historical novels. From these he turned to sporting topics. *My Shooting Box* (Philadelphia, 1843) dealt with game and game birds and went through four editions. It was reprinted in 1930 and 1931. Even more popular was *Frank Forester's Field Sports in the United States and British Provinces of North America* (London and New York, 1848) in two volumes. Again it was largely concerned with hunting game and birds, and it went through eleven editions. Herbert followed it with *Frank Forester's Fish and Fishing of the United States and British Provinces of North America* (London, 1849). It was issued the next year in New York and enjoyed as many editions as the previous work. Herbert also illustrated it. *American Game in its Season* (New York, 1853) was an anthology of articles he had contributed to *Graham's Magazine*.

Sports fans show limited interest in the origins of the games or contests they watch. They talk of recent victories or defeats they can recall, and it is always the coming season or event that stirs most excitement. Bibliographies of sports are not fully satisfactory. For complete coverage they are dependent upon examination of large private collections, and evidently these have not been found. Consequently there are discrepancies and lacunae in the histories of various sports. Academically, this field has not achieved acceptance, although an occasional social historian will pay some attention to the cultural aspects of these national enthusiasms. The full history of sports remains to be written.

CHAPTER TEN

Architecture in America

Plate from Benjamin's Practical House
Carpenter, *1830*

CHAPTER TEN

Architecture in America

RECONSTRUCTION of the Pilgrim village at Plymouth, Massachusetts, and the Jamestown settlement in Virginia has fully demonstrated that the first settlers did not live in log cabins. It was the Swedes and the Finns who settled on the Delaware who introduced those structures. On the frontier log cabins prevailed, for they could be built quickly by men without carpentry skills, and they were virtually costless. One- or two-room dwellings made of notched logs are not considered to have architectural claims. They were strictly utilitarian, not intended to be attractive, and the possibilities for design were negligible.

But the shops and dwellings that went up in the seventeenth century in Boston, Providence, Baltimore, Philadelphia, Charleston, and on southern plantations showed an earnest desire to reproduce architecture familiar to the immigrants from England. New York being of Dutch origin, its earliest buildings were in the Dutch style: narrow, three stories high with stepped gables, and some doors cut in two horizontally. Restored Williamsburg and some early surviving houses in Salem and Savannah make clear that in the eighteenth century Americans could construct some beautiful buildings.

Admittedly, American architecture was derivative for a long time. It was also delayed—about a generation behind the changing styles in England. Thus the so-called colonial architecture of the seventeenth century was Elizabethan in style, with traces of earlier Gothic influence. Houses were built around a huge central chimney, with two rooms downstairs and two up. A short hall permitted only an angular stairway. The second story overhung the first, and the roof was steep. Ceiling beams were visible, and small windows with small panes prevailed. The exterior was covered with narrow clapboards or shingles. The so-called Cape Cod cottage, a story and a half high, with or without dormer windows, was a variant of this style that survived to be built again and again in the eighteenth and nineteenth centuries. In the South, where red clay was common, bricks were used. When the house stood a story and a half high, still with four rooms, there was usually a chimney at either end.

Meanwhile, in England the Renaissance, inspired by Roman architectural forms, developed into a Baroque style of heavy ornamentation under the influence of Sir Christopher Wren and associated with the Stuart monarchs of the seventeenth century. In America this style appeared at the very end of the century and in the early eighteenth century in more elaborate houses and public buildings. We see its finest flowering, delayed, in Williamsburg and neighboring James River plantation houses like Westover and Carter's Grove. An occasional northern house reveals the Wren influence. Sometimes this style is called Early Georgian, since architectural historians do not agree on labels or periods.

Georgian architecture of eighteenth-century England was in the Palladian style derived from Andrea Palladio, Italian architect of the sixteenth century, as interpreted by Inigo Jones. It was taken up by Whig noblemen to show their opposition to the last Stuart monarchs and the Wren influence. But design books show that it did not reach America in its pure classical forms, but in simplified versions presented by such British architectural authors as James Gibbs, Abraham Swan, and others, who did not completely turn their backs on Wren's touches. They kept the symmetrical balance and proportions of the main block and the columns of the front doorways or porticos, but relieved the flat, severe wall planes with ornaments of quoins, pilasters, and balustrades and offered dependent structures, attached or not, on either side of the central block. Hence, the American Georgian style—sometimes called Late Georgian—was a subtle blend of Palladio and Wren. Balanced triple windows, with the center one the largest, became a Palladian trademark. The style caught on particularly in the South, but it spread up to Philadelphia and the New England seaports.

In houses this style was characterized by a central hall containing an elaborate stairway and generally two rooms on either side of the hall. A Palladian window above the front door lighted the upper stairhall. Paneled doors featured a broken pediment, windows were larger and regularly spaced, and two chimneys rose at each end of the houses. Paneling and heavy cornices decorated the rooms. Upstairs were four more rooms, and usually the roof was hipped. The facade was balanced, and obviously the house was designed from the outside in. The kitchen was frequently in a separate structure attached by hall or colonnade to the main house and balanced on the other side by a similar structure enclosing an office, library, or servant's room, as at Mt. Vernon. This arrangement approached the full Palladian villa. Sliding sash windows replaced casement windows. Narrow hardwood floors replaced the wide pine planks of colonial houses. In churches large rectangular buildings were favored, with a double row of windows, sometimes arched, to light the high one-story interior with its balconies held up by ornamented columns. The tall spires of several tiers rose heavenward above the entrance. Some of our earliest college buildings were Georgian.

Toward the end of the century the Georgian style merged into a purer Classical style of the Federal period. As the authority for Classical forms, Palladio was overthrown by archeological discoveries. Architects were left to choose which Classical order they would use. Symmetry was based on proportions mathematically conceived. The inverted V of the roof was low-pitched, the eaves were prominent and decorated, doorways showed elliptical fanlights, and there might be curved bays. This style was overtaken in turn by a Greek Revival early in the nineteenth century which was prominently American. It was noticed in Great Britain, but did not catch on there.

After building from memory in the seventeenth century, American carpenters and contractors eagerly turned to architectural books in the eighteenth and nineteenth centuries for designs and instructions. These plan books by British architects were widely imported. The extent of American familiarity with them was not realized until after the investigation completed in 1961 by Helen Park, who found 87 imported architectural books owned in the colonies before 1775. She revised and extended her bibliography in 1973 to include 106 titles. Her list does not mean that there was only one copy of each title available here, but often several copies, up to thirty-one. The magnificent plates in those big volumes show prototypes of American churches and houses. Designs by the popular William and John Halfpenny, James Gibbs, Batty Langley, Abraham Swan, and William Pain were most favored here, along with those by Sir William Chambers, William Salmon, Isaac Ware, and Robert Morris. They all celebrated the modified Palladian style.

Indeed, the first architectural work published in this country was a reprint of Abraham Swan's *The British Architect* (Philadelphia, 1775). The publisher, John Norman, who moved to America before the Revolution and became a talented engraver and printer, compiled from various English sources another work called *The Town and Country Builder's Assistant* (Boston, 1786). This was followed by four of William Pain's books in the 1790s. No American authors yet.

Another Englishman, a craftsman, enjoyed tremendous acceptance here. He was Peter Nicholson (1765–1844). His *The Carpenter's New Guide* first appeared in London in 1792. Thereafter, for eighty years it was constantly reprinted in England and the United States with little change. Among other techniques, it showed an original method of making handrails, groins, and niches. Nicholson issued a second handbook in 1824: *The Mechanic's Companion; or, the Elements and Practice of Carpentry, Joinery, Bricklaying, Masonry, Slating, Plastering, Painting, Smithing and Turning*. It was reprinted at least ten times in this country. Both books were liberally illustrated. According to architectural historian Talbot Hamlin, these two titles account for the "high standards of building construction and practical details in the use of materials" so evident in America in the first half of the nineteenth century. Indeed, said Hamlin, Nicholson "almost deserves to be called the father of American carpentry and joinery."

The problem in documenting architecture is that the most active architects in early America did not publish books of their own designs or write about their art. Peter Harrison of Newport, Charles Bulfinch of Boston, Samuel McIntire of Salem, Benjamin Latrobe of Baltimore, William Strickland of Philadelphia, John McComb, Jr., of New York, and Robert Mills of Charleston were responsible for many attractive public buildings and houses, but they are known by their creations, not by their writings. In addition, there were a dozen or more amateur architects who designed their own houses or one or two public buildings as a hobby: Richard Taliaferro and Thomas Jefferson of Virginia, Dr. John Kearsley and attorney Andrew Hamilton of Pennsylvania, William Buckland of Maryland, and Joseph Brown of Rhode Island.

It was left to the second echelon of practicing architects to publicize their designs and to borrow from the great English builders, in order to aid and educate the numerous contractors and carpenters in the States. Given drawings and proportions, those builders could tap the extraordinary craftsmanship of American woodworkers for moldings, paneling, staircases and balusters, mantels, columns and pilasters.

The first design book by an American was *The Country Builder's Assistant* (Greenfield, 1797), with thirty plates, by

Asher Benjamin (1773–1845), Boston architect and author. It was reprinted at Boston the following year, with thirty-seven plates. Benjamin copied designs from English authors, drew heavily on Charles Bulfinch, and offered detailed information to village carpenters. In the main his plans were in the Federal style. What distinguished him was his excellent taste. His *The American Builder's Companion* (Boston, 1806) ran through six editions, with the number of plates increasing from forty-four to seventy. *The Rudiments of Architecture* (Boston, 1814) was likewise popular. He moved toward more rigid Classicism and was largely responsible for popularizing the Greek Revival in *The Practical House Carpenter* (Boston, 1830), frequently reprinted. His revisions were marked by deletion of some material and addition of new.

Benjamin's enthusiasm for the Greek Revival style for churches, courthouse, and banks, as well as dwellings, was echoed by Chester Hills in *The Builder's Guide; or a Practical Treatise on the Several Orders of Grecian and Roman Architecture* (Hartford, 1834) in two volumes and seventy plates called "the most complete of any of the Greek Revival builder's guides." Three more editions were published. Many of his designs were borrowed. Neither man initiated the Greek Revival, but perhaps Benjamin Latrobe pointed the way with his building in Philadelphia for the Bank of Pennsylvania (1799), three years after he arrived from England. It was a Classical gem, and he did not hesitate to call himself a "bigoted Greek."

If Benjamin and Hills were dominant voices in the first half of the century, they were not the only ones. Owen Biddle produced *The Young Carpenter's Assistant; or, a System of Architecture Adapted to the Style of Building in the United States* (Philadelphia, 1805), the year before his early death. It contained many original designs. Although it was a tardy advocate of Palladian patterns, it was reprinted seven times over the next fifty years. This book makes clear that the Late Georgian style of Philadelphia had continuing appeal.

An English architect trained in London, John Haviland, migrated here in 1816, when he was twenty-four. Two years later he produced *The Builder's Assistant* in three volumes, with 150 plates which showed the Greek orders in detail for the first time. It was published in Philadelphia in 1818 to 1821. Among his Greek Revival plans, "copied from the antique," were sixty original designs. Haviland designed churches, public buildings, and houses. He also revised and enlarged Owen Biddle's book in 1833. Turning to something else, he designed prisons in a "radiating plan" that allowed easy supervision. Haviland built the Eastern State Penitentiary at Philadelphia and four other state prisons. Agents from foreign governments came to see them.

Minard Lafever of New York embraced the Greek Revival as ardently as Benjamin did, but was inspired to make original variations. His *The Young Builder's General Instructor* (Newark, 1829) contained a series of designs for doors, windows, and columns, plus a new Greek order of his own which was a variation on the Corinthian column. His second book, *The Modern Builder's Guide* (New York, 1833) still championed the Greek style and offered two house plans showing a temple with balanced wings. He emphasized Greek ornaments, and he brought columns indoors to mark room divisions. Lafever reached artistic maturity in *The Beauties of Modern Architecture* (New York, 1835), which was reprinted four times. His original crestings and pierced grills were a forerunner of iron porches and balconies. Yet he insisted that with no indigenous architecture, Americans were free to choose to build in any style—evidently, that is, of the past.

The fervent devotion to Greek Revival, modified though the original Greek forms were, spread from the East Coast through the Great Lakes and Mississippi Valley and into the South. In town after town there was harmony and aesthetic appeal in large and small houses, churches, courthouses, and college buildings, not to be seen again after the Civil War. Marshall Davidson believes that when Samuel F. Smith wrote the verses of *America* in 1832 and pictured the landscape of mountainside, rocks and rills, and "templed hills," he was referring to the Greek-style white dwellings visible everywhere. It was not hard to compare our institutions superficially with those of classical antiquity, although it was done with a variety of interpretations. In the North the style was witness to faith in democracy and learning. In the South it was a pleasant reminder that in ancient Greece a cultured aristocracy, still much admired, rested on slavery. This divergence of interpretation anticipated the disagreement that would lead to war.

In retrospect, the historian is more impressed that this was an age in America that seemed free and secure and confident. There was no sense of hopelessness and no looking to government for anything more than open opportunities. If there was wealth and poverty (though without the extremes seen in Europe), there was also a dominant middle class, and all strata were soft rather than rigid, and easily penetrated by anyone on the rise. With a similar glance backward to the seventeenth century in New England, Alan Gowans noted that "what had been withheld by inscrutable grace was being brought about by education in the classics. Arcadia had displaced Jerusalem as the American dream." Therefore, it seems foolish to argue that the Greek Revival was an artificial taste that did not symbolize American aspirations. Moreover, it was not confining to architects, who did not hesitate to make variations from it. Rather it was a climax to a long period of looking back to Classical models, and as a climax it would come rapidly to an end. The Civil War finished it off, and it had already suffered the appearance of a rival style in the Gothic Revival.

The Gothic Revival style was less expensive, and the plans offered were usually for smaller, more modest houses. In large public buildings the style was associated in some minds with European Christianity as seen in late medieval cathedrals. Some fine Gothic churches in cut stone were built in this country, and the movement appealed to colleges for its association with the buildings of Oxford and Cambridge universities.

The author of the first American book on landscape gardening, which became a classic after its appearance in 1841, was Andrew Jackson Downing, who soon ventured into architecture. *Cottage Residences* (New York, 1842) went through several editions, popularizing smaller houses of Gothic design, or what he called "cottage villas and their gardens and grounds." Downing enlarged on this style with *The Architecture of Country Houses* (New York, 1850) with 321 plans, of which 32 were original with him. It became one of the most influential pattern books in midcentury. He asserted that "the Greek temple disease has passed its crisis. The people have survived it." What he offered was simply another revival, with considerable modification and adulteration. It featured narrow windows, pointed or rounded at the top; vertical lines of board and batten siding, porches with thin square posts replacing columns, brackets under the cornices, and lattice work under the eaves—the "gingerbread" decoration cut by new jigsaws.

Downing's protégé, Calvert Vaux, whom he brought to this country from England, issued a similar work: *Villas and Cottages. A Series of Designs Prepared for Execution in the United States* (New York, 1857). It was revised and published thrice in the 1860s. His designs were more in the "stick style" of frame construction which revealed all kinds of projecting rooms and balconies in its planning of spaces from inside out. It seemed to be freer of any historical precedent.

The profession did not escape its eccentrics. Orson Fowler (1809–1887) was a college graduate, full of undigested knowledge in several fields, enormous conceit, zeal for reform, and no critical judgment. First he became an ardent phrenologist and then a fanciful physiologist. With this background he turned to housing and developed a bizarre notion that an eight-sided house would improve the health of its occupants and be easier to take care of. He wrote *A House for All; or, the Gravel Wall and Octagon Mode of Building* (New York, 1848), advocating masonry walls as a way of constructing a comfortable dwelling "within reach of the poorer classes." The octagon house, of masonry or wood siding, enjoyed a vogue all through the 1850s, but seldom were there more than one or two such houses to a town.

If the octagon house, while it lasted, was a unique American contribution to architectural design, two other developments distinguished American building and gave architects new freedom and new opportunities. Both occurred at approximately the same time, around 1830. One was the attention given to hotel construction, and the other was the so-called balloon frame for housing.

Before 1820 city hotels were, with few exceptions, crude, and accommodations anything but private or comfortable. On stagecoach routes between towns, overnight facilities were worse. On the frontier the traveler usually stayed in cabins with families not in the innkeeping business. After Boston's Exchange Hotel burned in 1818, some merchants and civic leaders sponsored a needed new hotel and awarded the architect's commission to Isaiah Rogers, a twenty-eight-year-old designer who had been trained in a local architectural office. With almost no models to follow, Rogers designed the Tremont House in 1828 as a four-story building with a granite front and colonnaded portico in the Greek Revival style. Inside were numerous public parlors, a central rotunda office, and a formal dining room with a screen of Ionic columns at either end. The public rooms were gaslit (a novelty); the bedrooms still had whale-oil lamps, but they had pushbuttons to the office to summon bellboy, porter, or chambermaid. Eight water closets were available on the first floor, and bathrooms were found in the basement. The hotel was depicted in William H. Eliot's *A Description of the Tremont House with Architectural Illustrations* (Boston, 1830), the year after it opened.

By the time Rogers completed the Astor House in New York in 1836, he was able to get plumbing above the ground so that every floor had its bathrooms and water closets, fed from a roof tank filled by a steam pump. In contrast to eighteenth-century inns, the pattern of elegance and splendor was set. Hotels blossomed everywhere, distinctive buildings in every city, shown with pride, and serving a restive, migratory people. Historian Daniel Boorstin perceived the role

played by hotels in community life and has written delightfully on the social effects of these "palaces of the public."
Their significance in American housing was that they became
testing places for the most advanced domestic conveniences,
and mechanical equipment required consideration in design.

The invention of the steam-powered circular saw about
1814 made it possible to slice logs into two-inch-thick slabs
of varying widths, and the ubiquitous two-by-four was born.
A nail-cutting machine reduced the cost of nails to one-fifth
that of handwrought nails. As a result, someone in Chicago
built a church in 1833 of two-by-twelve joists and two-by-
four partition studs. The method began to spread quickly.
The old style of house building was post and beam construction; that is, heavy square beams, about ten by ten or larger,
were fitted to upright posts of the same size by making a hole
in the post to accommodate a tenon, or shaved end, of a
beam. To make sure the joint would not pull loose, another
hole was drilled with an auger and a wooden peg pounded
into the joined timbers. They were braced by smaller posts.
The fitting of beams required the skills of a competent carpenter, and there were simply not enough of them in Chicago
to meet demand. The new style of framing could be nailed
together by almost anyone. Consequently it was derided as a
"balloon frame" or "Chicago construction." The one epithet
was meant to imply frailty, and the other, cheapness. The first
was false, for the balloon frame was unusually strong from its
tensions, and the whole was stronger than its parts, whereas
heavy beams were often weakened by the holes made in them
for posts and cross beams. Undeniably, the new technique
was a cheaper method of construction, and that is why it
became so popular, until it is found everywhere today. Further it permitted the taking down of houses to move them and
encouraged the manufacture of prefabricated houses, or the
lumber for them, which could be shipped in parts by boat or
wagon or railroad freight car. On the architect's drawing
board, windows and doors could be shifted about, the traditional rectangular house could be changed in shape, and

dormers, projections, and additions were relatively easy. Thus before the Civil War, planning and building were beginning to be freed of traditional limitations.

In architecture the historian finds the impact and influence of several developments in other fields. First of all, there is an intellectual discovery: the fact that there is no evolution in art; design does not "improve" century by century. It changes according to taste, and a period of good taste is followed by a period of bad taste, either one difficult to explain. Outside events do affect expressions of that taste. Thus the excavations of Pompeii and Herculaneum in the late eighteenth century, followed by the Greek revolution, undoubtedly contributed to the Classical and Greek revivals. Other external factors influence design. House taxes once levied according to windows limited their number. Outside or detached kitchens were brought inside after stoves replaced fireplaces for cooking. Expense of land in major cities forced buildings to go higher and higher. Municipal zoning regulates what can be built.

Technological development was quickly transferred to architectural consideration, such as new tools (like power saws and balloon framing, jigsaws and decoration), furnaces for central heating, elevators, new building materials, improved lighting fixtures, central sewer and water connections, kitchen appliances, fireproofing methods—indeed, the whole business of local government building codes. Any improvement in the standard of living showed up immediately in better housing, because houses reflect how people think about themselves. In this sense architecture is a mirror and a measuring device for the social historian.

CHAPTER ELEVEN

To the Aspiring Collector

A New York collector's vault, ca. 1920.
From A. S. W. Rosenbach, Books and Bidders
(Boston: Little, Brown and Company, 1927); courtesy of the
Rosenbach Museum and Library, Philadelphia.

CHAPTER ELEVEN

To the Aspiring Collector

HE FOREGOING CHAPTERS mention some of the books basic to early American history that were sought and saved by earlier generations of collectors. Enough hints have been dropped to indicate that whenever copies of them do become available, they are costly, often beyond the reach of everyone except the very rich—individuals, institutions, or investors. Is Americana collecting becoming an extinct pursuit, something like hunting buffalo, which can no longer be practiced?

The outlook is not so bleak. Americana of some kind is still the choice of a majority of book collectors in our country today. It was not always so. Book collecting began with a primary interest in the Greek and Roman classics—poetry, drama, philosophy, orations, science, history. Often they were incunabula: books printed before 1500. Another favorite field was examples of the first books printed in various European countries and cities. Then came a desire for literary masterpieces of the western world, especially English literature. Americana was disdained as a minor, provincial interest, hardly challenging to serious collectors, until about the middle of the nineteenth century.

If any one person may be credited with stimulating this interest and making it respectable, it was Henry Stevens of

Vermont. In pursuit of early books on America, this Yale graduate migrated to London in 1848 and remained there until his death in 1886. He arrived in time to help the British Museum expand its library on the New World, and he served the Library of Congress similarly. Stevens was joined in 1860 by his brother, Benjamin F. Stevens, but in a few years the latter set up for himself and became an agent for the United States libraries. He also copied manuscripts in British depositories for the Library of Congress and published in twenty-four volumes copies of manuscripts in foreign archives relating to America from 1763 to 1783.

Meanwhile, Henry Stevens, becoming expert in the geographical and historical literature of the New World, advised such collectors as John Carter Brown of Providence, James Lenox of New York, and George Brinley, Jr., of Hartford. These three men, above all others, made Americana an esteemed and exciting field for collecting. A few minor collectors had added a little Americana, often of regional scope, to their libraries. A small wind across this field was raised by a few Eastern historical societies which collected books on the origins and early history of their own states. The American Antiquarian Society of Worcester, Massachusetts, tried to collect general Americana, including much family history.

Brown's son continued his father's collecting until in 1900 he turned over their fruits to trustees, who later gave the splendid collection to Brown University. The John Carter Brown Library continues in the pattern of the founder. Lenox, who was first interested in Bibles, incunabula, and Shakespeare, opened the doors of the Lenox Library in 1870. Stevens wrote *Recollections* about him in 1886. In 1895 the Lenox Library, the Astor Library of reference books, and the Tilden Trust were combined to form the New York Public Library. Brinley's more than 10,000 volumes were dispersed at auction in sales running from 1879 to 1893, called "the first great book sale in this country." Brown and Lenox bought at the first sales, as did lesser collectors and dealers.

The book business of Henry Stevens was carried on by his son, Henry N. Stevens, until his death in 1930. He was aided early on by the Columbian Exposition, or Chicago World's Fair, of 1893. This lively and popular fair, among its other effects, stimulated a new interest among historians and bibliographers in Columbus and other voyages of discovery. Book dealers in this country found it worthwhile to specialize almost exclusively in Americana. Early in this century such firms as Goodspeed's of Boston; George D. Smith, Lathrop Harper, and Edward Eberstadt of New York; Wright Howes of Chicago; and John Howell of San Francisco funneled rare Americana into the hands of the increasing number of collectors.

Those dealers found books for such Americanists as William L. Clements, Henry E. Huntington, William R. Coe, Thomas W. Streeter, Everett Graff, Tracy McGregor, and others. These collectors sought to cover broad periods of American history with varying emphases. What affects the market today is that, with one partial exception, their books passed into libraries, greatly diminishing the available supply for others. The Clements collection went to the University of Michigan, the Huntington collection to the institution bearing its founder's name in California, the Coe books of western Americana to Yale, the Graff collection to the Newberry Library in Chicago, and the McGregor books to the University of Virginia. Only Mr. Streeter, after adding his Texas collection to Yale's library, specified in his will that his remaining books be auctioned for the benefit of other collectors and libraries. Seven sales were held from 1966 to 1969. Thus the supply of older Americana has grown excessively scarce.

Meanwhile, two great bibliographies appeared, to guide all collectors of Americana. In his *American Bibliography* Charles Evans listed all books printed in America before 1801, in twelve volumes. They were published from 1903 to 1934; two more volumes carrying through 1800 appeared in 1969. Altogether they contain about 40,000 entries. A more ambitious work was begun by Joseph Sabin, a rare-book dealer who was auctioneer for the early Brinley sales, entitled *Dictionary of Books Relating to America*. Sabin sought to include all books, regardless of where they were published, printed before about 1860. The first volume appeared in 1868, but Sabin completed only fourteen volumes before he died in 1881. The project was carried on by Wilberforce Eames and finished by R. W. G. Vail in 1936, in twenty-nine volumes. The set contains more than 106,000 entries. Various special bibliographies have also appeared, listing Americana by topics, by regions, and by authors. They, too, serve as guides for collectors. Further, a make-work project late in the Depression decade was the Federal Imprints Inventory, which published a list of books printed in each state during its early years. Forgotten imprints were rediscovered, and order given to those particular titles. The Inventories may be consulted at libraries.

Probably it is now too late for anyone to duplicate the extensive collections of early Americana of the magnitude of the collectors already named. For one thing, most of the old dealers are gone: Smith and Eberstadt and Howes are closed; Lathrop Harper's business, in other hands, goes on in a much broader vein; Goodspeed and Howell continue under new generations. The Stevens firm was carried on by another Henry Stevens and Roland Tree until their deaths, and now Henry Stevens, Son & Stiles functions in Farnham, Surrey, and Larchmont, New York. Of course, several new dealers are handling more modern Americana today, a recognition that many of the early key pieces can no longer be found. Even lesser sixteenth- and seventeenth-century titles may be out of reach. In the eighteenth century sermons and later editions of political tracts are still available at reasonable prices. The nineteenth century is fairly wide open, except for two or three expensive American authors and sources for the westward movement. In the twentieth century a few subjects are costly—such authors as O'Neill, Faulkner, Hemingway, and a few items in science—but in the whole period since 1865 scholars are still panning the source materials for the most significant nuggets. Collectors participate in this process, too, for the most important titles in politics, literature, economics, warfare, religion, education, science, music, and the like have not been identified and agreed upon.

The amateur collector with limited funds need not feel excluded from the game. He can buy facsimiles or reprints of the elusive old rarities, but that is not considered respectable collecting. Neither is the gathering of later editions. It is better if he sharpens his wits by investigating a more recent topic of particular interest to him and becomes knowledgeable enough to make discriminating judgments. He must reflect on what he learns. He may collect on a particular period, even as small as the Depression decade or a presidential administration, or on a region or state, a political movement, a religious enthusiasm, an invention, space exploration, a shaping idea such as the energy shortage, an influential individual, an important food or fiber, or a neglected author he believes will endure. He may identify a trend that will become significant in retrospect. What has helped shape our country in recent decades? What are the dominant characteristics of America today, and which books reveal them? The possibilities seem infinite.

Most historical studies and biographies (secondary works) carry a list of sources consulted, thus enabling a collector to start his own bibliographical guide. In collecting, almost always "one thing leads to another." Book dealers are always glad to help by drawing on their enormous experience with books, and they are pleased to send their catalogs to beginning collectors. They can be found in the advertisements of *A. B. Bookman's Weekly* (the initials stand for *Antiquarian Bookman,* the first name of the periodical) and in the *Papers* (actually a quarterly magazine) of the Bibliographical Society of America. The membership list of the Antiquarian Booksellers' Association of America is printed in the appendix to S. J. Iacone's *The Pleasures of Book Collecting* (New York, 1976), each member indicating his specialty.

Catalogs of book auctions are available on subscription. There are three houses active in New York City: Sotheby Parke Bernet, Christie's, and Swann Gallery. The first two have lately introduced the European custom of charging a commission to all buyers. Occasionally there are Americana auctions in other cities; in California they are held alternately in San Francisco and Los Angeles. Often items of Americana are mixed in with other books. To participate in a book auction it is advisable to employ a local dealer and pay him a commission.

Collecting is a quest and provides all the excitement of a chase. The collector in a real sense endeavors to complete a design that has formed in his mind, as an artist might. He also becomes a connoisseur in his chosen field. As the early mist that overhangs his interest rises, the fun begins.

Index